PETRA

JORDAN'S EXTRAORDINARY ANCIENT CITY

BARNES
&NOBLE
BOOKS
NEW YORK

To the Jordanian People

PETRA

ART, HISTORY AND ITINERARIES IN THE NABATEAN CAPITAL

Texts by
Fabio Bourbon

Translation
Barbara Fisher

EnglishTranslation
Editor
Dough Lloyd

Graphic Design
Clara Zanotti
Paola Piacco

Maps and drawings
Monica Falcone Bourbon
Fabio Bourbon

CONTENTS

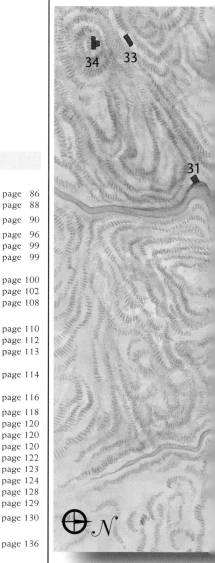

34   33

31

N

© 2004 White Star S.r.l.
Via Candido Sassone, 22/24
13100 Vercelli, Italy.

This edition published by
Barnes & Noble, Inc., by
arrangement with White Star S.r.l.

2004 Barnes & Noble Books

ISBN 0-7607-5619-8
M 10987654321
Printed in China by Midas Printing

The publishers wish to thank:
Royal Jordanian,
Jordan Tourism Board of Amman,
Intercontinental Hotel of Amman, and
Petra Forum Rest House, for their invaluable
assistance with the preparation of this book.

Cover
The Khasneh.
(© A. Attini / Archivio White Star)
Back cover:
*Top left - The Deir in a
lithograph by David Roberts.*
(© Library of Congress, Prints
and Photographs Division,
Washington)

Top right - The Urn Tomb.
(© M. Borchi / Archivio White Star)
*Centre - The front of the temple
known as Kasr el Bint.*
(© Monica and
Fabio Bourbon)
*Bottom - A male bust of a
divinity, identified as Serapis.*
(© M. Borchi / Archivio White Star)

1 The Bab el Siq
Triclinium and the
Obelisk Tomb above it
are two prime examples
of Nabatean
monumental rock
architecture.

2-3 In this stunning
photograph, the top of
the Deir – or Monastery
– emerges like part of a
surreal stage set from
behind the rocky ridges
that surround Petra.

In the presence of such a
spectacle it is easy to
understand why, even
in antiquity, the Rock
City enjoyed an
extraordinary
reputation.

4 Mountains of
multicolored sandstone,
the most typical landscape
in Petra and the
surrounding region, were
fashioned by the erosive
action of the elements.

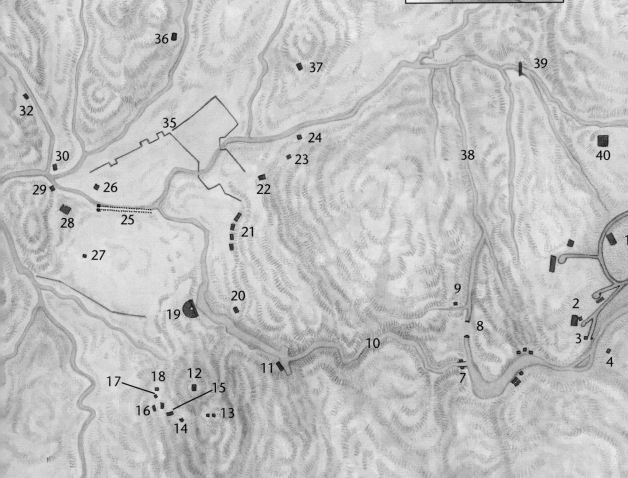

LEGEND

1 Wadi Mousa
2 Petra Forum Rest House
3 Entrance Gate
4 Brooke Hospital
5 Djin Blocks
6 Obelisk Tomb and Bab el SiqTriclinium
7 Triumphal Arch
8 Nabatean Tunnel

9 Eagle Monument
10 Siq
11 Khasneh
12 High Place of Sacrifice
13 Obelisks
14 Lion Monument
15 Garden Tomb
16 Roman Soldier Tomb and Triclinium

17 Renaissance Tomb
18 Broken Pediment Tomb
19 Theatre
20 Tomb of Uneishu
21 Royal Tombs
22 Tomb of Sextius Florentinus
23 Carmine Façade
24 House of Dorotheus
25 Colonnade Street

26 Temple of the Winged Lions
27 Pharaoh Column
28 Kasr el Bint
29 Old Museum
30 New Museum
31 Quarry
32 Lion Triclinium
33 El Deir
34 Monument 468
35 City walls

36 Turkamaniya Tomb
37 Armor Tomb
38 Little Siq
39 Aqueduct
40 Crusader Castle of al Wu'aira

INTRODUCTION

The ruins of Petra constitute one of the most extraordinary and fascinating monumental complexes of the ancient world for the outstanding quality of the architecture and for the city's remarkable position among rugged hills and narrow gorges. Further charm is added by the color of the rock the buildings were built into. Petra is without doubt one of the marvels of the world, a place that will captivate even the most hardened traveller, one of those places that you never forget, not even years later. How strange that, in the era of the "global village", with distances cancelled by the Internet, mass media and millions of pictures of the farthest corners of the globe, there is still something that can astound technological man. Petra does this and without difficulty. Photographic reports on this

sensational part of Jordan appear regularly in magazines and specialist journals, dozens of documentaries have described its splendor, and even those least susceptible to the charms of archaeology have seen it thanks to film director Steven Spielberg, as some of the most spectacular scenes in the film "Indiana Jones and the Last Crusade" were set in Petra.

So, Petra ought to surprise no one, least of all the well-prepared tourist, who reads every available guidebook before setting off and thinks he knows all there is to know. But, once he or she is actually *there*, even the hardest materialist will be overwhelmed by emotion.

What really takes everyone by surprise is its *dimension*, not merely in terms of surface area occupied by the archaeological site. Petra is, indeed, far larger than can be imagined, but this is not the point. The rock structures are also colossal and, at the end of the day, visitors return to their hotels with stiff necks caused by looking up all the time; but not even this justifies the sense of wonder produced by the Rose-red City.

It is the *dimension* entered as soon as you pass through the gate, a perception of space and time that is different from what you are accustomed to. As well as being an actual location, Petra is a place of the mind. In Petra proportions seem inexplicably different, time flows at a different pace, the very air seems to take on a new consistency. Nothing is more agonizingly beautiful than that moment, at dusk, when the sunbeams flood the great carved rock façades with light and the rock itself creates a kaleidoscope of colors unequalled anywhere on the multicolored surface of the Earth.

In Petra, a sense of the fantastic is normal.

In Petra the word *impossible* has no meaning.

6 left The photograph shows the huge tholos of the Deir, one of the most stunning and best-preserved monuments in Petra.

6 top right Although the combined action of wind and water have undermined their original splendour, Petra's monuments preserve unequalled majesty. Here you can see a detail of the Palace Tomb.

6 bottom right The perfect symbiosis between the glowing colors of the stone and the structural fantasy of its ancient creators makes Petra a unique archaeological site.

7 The contrast between the delightfully shady Siq and the façade of the Khasneh, bathed in warm, golden light, is perhaps what most thrills visitors to the ancient Nabatean city.

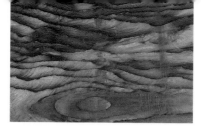

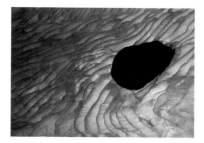

In Petra, Mother Nature has achieved one of its most original creations: improbable geometry, unbelievable colors, contrasts that would be unthinkable elsewhere.

However, all this fails to explain the magic of Petra, for Petra is one of the few places in the world where the work of man has completed the work of creation with complete harmony and grace. The Nabateans, who were responsible for this extraordinary miracle, did not violate nature, they conformed to it, adapting and indulging it with the utmost elegance. This is what makes Petra unique.

A Gothic cathedral, a mosque, a Hindu temple are constructions of man that often assert, even more than the glory of God, the conceit and power of their builders. They are *made* of stone taken *from* the ground, and rise *above* its surface, interfering with the earth's natural balance. Men, by their very nature, tend to alter the world around them. However, in Petra, all that has been built is one with, and inseparable from, the rock itself.

They built huge monuments to celebrate their civilization, but they did so with unequalled discretion and sensitivity. One could argue that the Nabateans also wanted to leave a proud mark of their passage on this planet, but there is a huge difference between what they did and what has been and still is the norm elsewhere. Although the centuries that will pass

The manmade structures extend and complete the natural formations, making sense of the lines of force that run beneath the crazily wrinkled surface of the stone and turn it into pure art. Two thousand years before Alvar Aalto, Frank Lloyd Wright and the appearance of the very concept of "organic architecture," the Nabateans succeeded in a matchless undertaking: They managed to create a total and successful balance between the needs of civilized life and the laws of nature.

before erosion eliminates all traces of Petra, may seem like an eternity, they are a mere blip in the flow of geological time.

When the concerted action of wind, water and sun has completed its task, not a trace of Petra will remain: not a ruin, not a carved block, the cavities will have turned into caves or been reduced to fissures, gorges will become openings indistinguishable from the surrounding delirium of natural form. The earth's surface will regain its pure

and primitive appearance. Even in death – in its long, sweet, inevitable death – Petra is an organic part of the mountains that surround it and of which it is made. This is what makes it so fascinating and this is why we ask anyone wishing to visit it to do so with respect. Nothing is more irritating or annoying than to hear the shouts and yells of insensitive people who come here and act as if at the stadium or on the streets of a modern metropolis.

8 and 9 Inside, the tombs of Petra usually consist of large totally unadorned rooms, with pits or wall niches of varying sizes, which contained the dead. Whether or not they were originally plastered and decorated remains open to debate; some underground rooms still frescoed in Wadi Siyagh and el Barid would suggest this, but many believe that the Nabatean builders usually preferred to exploit the natural veining of the sandstone, to surprising effect. Certainly, the color combinations of the rocks are of matchless beauty.

Leave no trace of your passage, leave no litter or cans and make no more noise than is necessary. Respect the mysterious sacredness of this place and do so in tribute to those who devotedly and lovingly keep vigil over this masterpiece. In return, Petra will give you its charm. Take your time, look for a quiet spot and listen to the poetry of silence, look around, observe the changing colors, corners created by shadows on rock walls and on sculpted stone façades. Take a deep breath of the dry air, feel intoxicated by such abounding splendor, fill your eyes with beauty, and be moved. If you do not believe in magic then you will have to change your mind. When you go home, a treasure will be stored deep down in your heart.

HISTORY

DAMASCUS

SUEIDA

JERASH · BOSRA

JERUSALEM · AMMAN
GAZA · EIN GEDI · MADABA
EL HARISH · KARAK
MAMSHIT
ADVAT
PETRA

AQABA

RUWWAFA

RED SEA

HEGRA

ravelling from Amman along the modern but extremely monotonous Desert Road, or along the older and more spectacular King's Road, after a wide bend you will come across the first powerful vista of the stunning mountains that lovingly embrace and conceal the ancient Nabatean capital. You are at a height of approximately 3,280 feet, on the edge of a great depression, the lowest point of which (at approximately 1,312 feet below sea level is the lowest point on earth) is occupied by that geological oddity known as the Dead Sea. On the horizon, hidden from view by a striking number of towers fashioned by the wind, opens the great fault called Wadi Arabah, along which the Jordan River used to flow into the Gulf of Aqaba. Extending as far as the eye can see is a phantasmagoric succession of fine sandstone rocks worn smooth by erosion. Some are reddish and pockmarked with thousands of irregular holes; others, round, polished and white, look like huge, surreal skulls. Opening between one mountain and the other are deep drops steeped in shadow, their darkness a striking contrast to the blinding sunlight reflecting off the limestone peaks. The spectacle is breathtaking.

Before us lies the spacious valley in which stands the modern village of Wadi Mousa, dotted with comfortable hotels. Nothing would suggest that hidden a few miles away is the hollow in which the legendary Petra once flourished. Yet, it was this very "invisibility" – combined with the hostile and barren region around it – that for centuries guaranteed the safety and prosperity of the Rose-red City.

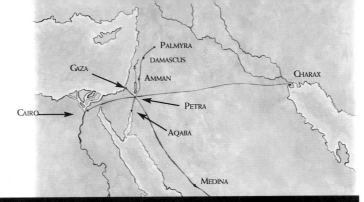

10 top *The map shows the position of Petra and the other main settlements in the region.*

10 bottom *The Nabatean culture was initially aniconical: Sculptures, reliefs and other representations are therefore expressions of an imported art.*

11 top *As shown on this map, Petra was situated in a highly strategic position; quick connections via the Red Sea allowed profitable communications with Arabia and Mesopotamia, while the route through the Negev Desert to Gaza guaranteed an outlet on the Mediterranean and access to the ports of Syria.*

10-11 *Petra valley was permanently inhabited from approximately 1500 BC until the Arab conquest, and countless traces of this long occupation remain. This quern for grinding corn is just one example.*

11 bottom *The numerous rock inscriptions found in and around Petra prove that the language spoken by the Nabateans was of Aramaic origin.*

Situated in southern Jordan, approximately 190 miles south of Amman, Petra is repeatedly mentioned in the Bible with the name of "Sela" (rock in Hebrew), whereas the Arabs called it Wadi Mousa, or "Valley of Moses;" the oldest local name for the city is still unknown. Petra is simply the Greek translation of the Biblical toponym. Although their name will always be bound to that of Petra, the Nabateans were not the first inhabitants of this place. During the Paleolithic period, the entire region was inhabited by groups of hunters and food gatherers who roamed endlessly in search of game and edible plants. Finds made by archaeologists prove that from 9000 BC on, during the Neolithic period, small communities given over to farming and the rearing of domestic animals settled here. A settlement that can be dated to this period in history has been found at el Beidha, situated slightly north of Petra.

During the Aeneolithic period and the subsequent Bronze Age (between 4000 and 2500 BC) in the region there were villages that lived off farming – therefore inhabited by stable populations – and camps of nomads, essentially devoted to sheep-rearing and thus ever on the move because of the constant need to find new land for grazing.

Later, at an as yet undetermined time, the villages of southern Jordan were abandoned for reasons linked perhaps with a worsening climate, and only the settlements of nomad tents survived and are known to have been present until the seventh century BC.

At a time fixed today at around 1500 BC – about the middle of the Bronze Age – the Bible states that the Orite people settled in the valley of Petra, inhabiting the numerous caves set in the sides of the mountains.

The Orites were subsequently

driven away by the Edomites, a people of Semitic stock, who came to occupy the lands between the Gulf of Aqaba and the Dead Sea around the 13th century BC. The Edomites claimed to be direct descendants of Esau, thus belonging to the same dynastic line as Moses. Despite this, when Moses, with the people of Israel, reached the borders of the kingdom of Edom, he was denied permission to cross the territory to reach the Promised Land. This story, however, was recorded in the Old Testament by the descendants of Moses and consequently, subsequent judgements regarding the Edomites (all negative) must be considered biased and not very reliable. Although the Bible is of questionable historic value, the relationships between the Israelites and Edomites are known to have been very bad for several centuries. After the fall of Jerusalem at the hands of the Babylonians in 587 BC, the inhabitants of Edom repeatedly attacked the kingdom of Judah. It must, however, be stressed that the Edomites themselves were under increasing pressure from a nomadic

people of Aramaic stock from the Arabian Peninsula who would soon oust them completely.

The Nabateans are first mentioned (with certainty as older evidence is considered controversial) in a historic document dating from the fourth century BC, although their arrival in the area had clearly started much earlier as they were driven north by Babylonian expansionism. Described as inhabitants of the desert, given over to sheep-rearing and ignorant of farming, "they built no houses nor drank any wine." Harsh, determined and resourceful, they managed to survive in the hostile climate of the Arabian desert thanks to the custom of digging large cisterns in the solid rock; the rare rainwater was channelled into the cisterns and conserved during the driest months. Their prosperity derived from

control of the caravan routes between Arabia and the Mediterranean, and those between Egypt and Mesopotamia and this control was maintained after they had settled in Petra.

In the early centuries of the Nabatean settlement, at least, Petra was very different from the splendid metropolis it was later to become; it consisted basically of a huge, disorganized camp of tents similar to those of present-day Bedouin families. Part of the population (still semi-nomadic) had to live in the numerous natural caves that opened in the uneven sides of the surrounding hills. The mountain of Umm al Biyara – called Petra, *the rock*, by the Greeks and which later gave the city its name – served as a stronghold in the event of enemy attack: Not surprisingly, numerous remains and some huge cisterns have been found on the top of it. Thanks to the strategic position in which the settlement had developed, the Nabateans made a living supplying water and food to the caravans, imposing a sort of levy and trading the most remunerative commodities themselves. Around the mid-fourth century BC, the Nabateans were becoming increasingly rich from the trade of spices, silver, frankincense and myrrh. Perched on the top of Umm al Biyara, in 321 BC, they managed to drive back an attack mounted by Antigonus I Monophtalmus (one of Alexander the Great's generals, who became king of a Hellenistic state), sanctioning their independence. Over the following 150 years, Petra succeeded in cheating the expansionist aims of Ptolemaic Egypt and Seleucid Syria, continuing to prosper. Because of the lack of written documents, this period remains rather obscure, although it is

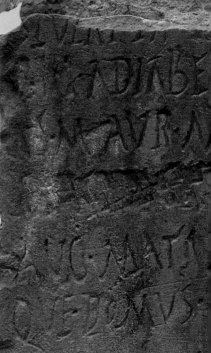

clear that the Nabateans were growing increasingly sedentary. Little by little, tents were replaced with houses, built along the bed of the Wadi Mousa and the camp was turned into a proper town.

The decline of the Hellenistic kingdoms coincided with the rise of Nabatean power, now backed by a solid monarchy. The first sovereign known by name was Aretas and he is mentioned in the second book of the Maccabees in connection with an episode that occurred around 168 BC. His successors included Aretas II (115-96 BC) and Obodas I (96-86 BC) who continued his expansionistic policy at the expense, in particular, of the Seleucid kingdom. In 85 BC, Aretas III (86-62 BC) even occupied Damascus. By the first century BC the Nabatean trade network had grown to include a number of caravan stations spread over a vast

12 left The Nabateans
lacked a figurative
tradition of their own, so
sculptures found in Petra,
such as this eagle, were
either imported from the
Greek-Roman world or
produced by local
workshops but based on
western iconography.

12 top
This panel adorned
with a male head
(perhaps the god
Ares) was found
with others near the
monumental three-
vault gate; all depict
deities of the Greek-
Roman pantheon.

12-13 Some Latin
inscriptions have been
found in Petra. Having
entered the sphere of
Roman influence as early
as the first century BC, the
Nabatean kingdom was
subjugated by Trajan in
106, apparently without
bloodshed.

13 right This splendid
relief, portraying a
young woman with a
veiled head and wearing
a diadem (almost
certainly the goddess
Aphrodite) betrays the
influence exercised by
Hellenism on local
artists.

area, from Hegra (today Madain Saleh,
in Saudi Arabia) to the towns of Negev,
Oboda, Mampsis and Sobata (today's
Advat, Mamshit and Shivta, in Israel).
Actually, the extensive area that
constituted the Nabatean kingdom had
no precise boundaries, as these depended
mainly on the military supremacy that
each sovereign managed to assert over
bordering states. In general terms, it
stretched from the south of modern
Syria to the Gulf of Aqaba, including the
Negev, Sinai, Trans-Jordan and part of
Arabia, as far as Hegra. Communities
of Nabatean merchants settled in major
ports of the East (Sidon) and West
(Pozzuoli, near Naples), and in Rome.
    Although difficult, relations with
the Jewish world were essentially
marked by policies of non-aggression;
during the same period, the

Nabateans managed for a long time to maintain total independence from the growing Roman power.

Petra – which the Nabateans called Reqem – had in the meanwhile expanded into the vast hollow between the mountains of Umm el Biyara and Jebel el Khubtha, where the Wadi Mousa, Wadi Mataha and Wadi Turkamaniya flow into a single seasonal river, Wadi Siyagh. The decision to make it the capital (perhaps made after the first friction with Rome) was motivated by safety requirements, as it was an ideal place of refuge hidden in the mountains with just a few easily controlled entrance routes.

Ongoing relations with the leading trading groups and increasing prosperity made it extremely cosmopolitan, which is particularly evident in the numerous monuments that the Nabatean kings had hewn into the rock walls around the city. Petra was enriched, in just a few decades, by artistic contributions from Syria, Egypt and the Hellenistic world and synthesized very different architectural and decorative canons into

14-15 Urban Petra consisted of raised constructions, but because of the earthquakes little more than the rock structures have survived.

14 bottom The Nabateans surrounded Petra with open-air sanctuaries where they venerated their gods. This is a detail of such a sanctuary on Jebel Attuf.

a unique formal language.

At the height of its splendor, the city must have numbered between 30 and 40 thousand inhabitants, most of them occupied in trade. For more than 200 years from the first century BC on, the public buildings became increasingly imposing in appearance. Great temples, markets and palaces were built along the city's main street, running from east to west. Of these, only Kasr el Bint has survived, and this tetrastyle temple is the only fairly well-preserved raised structure remaining in the whole of Petra. The reign of Aretas IV (8 BC - 40 AD) in particular constituted a golden era for monumental building; the construction of the so-called Great Temple and numerous other rearrangements of the urban fabric were designed to make Petra a worthy capital for the wealthy and famous Nabatean people.

Such prosperity, however, concealed a fundamental military weakness. The Roman civil wars had already posed a considerable danger to the stability of Petra. Aretas II, who had in 65 BC laid siege to Jerusalem, was forced to retreat before the legions of Pompey. Even worse, one of the Roman general's lieutenants then besieged Petra, although without managing to take it. In order to maintain their independence, the Nabateans agreed to pay tributes to Rome, thus becoming a client state.

The tax situation worsened considerably after Malchus I (59-30 BC) allied with the Parthians in their disastrous campaign against the Romans. In subsequent years it was again the Romans who further debilitated Nabatean power by tracing new trade routes through Arabia and relegating Petra to an ever-more-marginal position.

Therefore, the peaceful and prosperous reign of Aretas IV represented the culmination and, at the same time, the "swan song" of the Nabatean civilization. The last Nabatean king, Rabbel II (70-106 AD), perhaps having sensed what was about to happen, decided to transfer the capital to the north, to Bozrah. Despite the kingdom's continuing prosperity, the picture was changing rapidly. The Roman troops proceeded on their expansionist marches to conquer Syria, Judea and Egypt, tightening their grip on Petra. The end came suddenly and probably with no great shedding of blood. In 106 AD, the Emperor Trajan ordered his troops into the city and Petra was annexed to the province of Arabia.

Roman occupation was accomplished by sending an imperial legate to the city, which slowed down Petra's evolution, although without halting it entirely. Building continued, but as other caravan centers such as Jerash and Palmyra flourished its importance gradually diminished. For some centuries the Rock City resolutely lived on as a fairly active trading center; after the re-organization of the empire decided in 293 by Diocletian, it became the capital of the province of Palaestina Taertia. With the penetration of Christianity it rose to the status of an episcopal see and in the Byzantine period still enjoyed a certain prosperity; at the same time, numerous Nabatean rock structures were turned into Christian churches. After the 551 earthquake and the Arab conquest of the region, which took place in 663, Petra declined completely, although for a brief period in the 12th century it was fortified and defended by the crusaders, who called it Li Vaux Moise, the "Valley of Moses."

15 top This altar, standing approximately six and a half feet high, is sculpted in the rock of Jebel al Deir. High places were particularly sacred to the Nabateans, whose most important deities were Dusares and Al Uzza.

15 center and bottom Originally nomads, the Nabateans probably first started work on the rock structures in the third century BC, although the lack of written documents makes this date uncertain. Petra really started to develop as a city in the middle of the first century BC.

PETRA OF THE NABATEANS

*16 top and bottom
Although it is often
hard to identify the
actual function of
hypogea known not to
have been tombs, many
were certainly
dwellings. Most of
these are grouped into
districts on the
mountain slopes
overlooking the center
of the city, but many
are also found along
Wadi Mataha and
Wadi Siyagh.*

The site of the ancient Nabatean capital is shaped like an amphitheater enclosed within high rock faces; it measures approximately one mile across from east to west and just over a mile from north to south. The bed of an often-dry river, Wadi Mousa, crosses this wide valley and, with its tributaries, circumscribes two low rocky plateaus on which used to lie the city proper, later swept away by earthquakes and disastrous floods. The Nabateans are known to have settled here because of the location's easily defended position. All the ancient writers from Diodorus Siculus to Strabo and Pliny the Elder agree on this point. Initially Petra must have looked like a vast camp of tents, the inhabitants of which, in the event of danger, took refuge on the impregnable peaks all around; in fact, the first ring of walls dates only from the first century BC. Favored by its geographical position, Petra became the hub of a profitable herb, spice and other luxury goods trade and soon became rich. Permanent dwellings built with stones and mortar appeared as early as the

frames, imitating architectural views or showing vegetable motifs.

What boosted Petra's rapid urban development was the presence of perennial water springs in the area, although these soon became inadequate for the growing population. The Nabateans therefore designed a highly complex system of cisterns and channels dug into the rock, aqueducts running through clay pipes, dams and artificial basins, in which the rainwater was collected. With their hydraulic engineering they managed to satisfy the needs of a metropolis that grew to at least 30,000 inhabitants and was situated in a desert area where the rainfall does not exceed six inches per year. In the first century BC, the Nabatean capital was an affluent city (it would later become opulent), at the crossroads of major trade routes. Filling the void left by the decline of Greece, Petra set out to dominate militarily and economically a vast area of the Middle East while, at the same time, absorbing extremely mixed cultural and artistic influences and acquiring uncommonly refined tastes. As well as trade, the inhabitants of Petra dedicated themselves to shepherding, breeding dromedaries and cultivating wheat, for which they created huge terraces on the heights around the city. No longer nomads, the Nabateans had organized a hereditary monarchy, which wielded military and perhaps also religious power, without being strongly conditioned by the latter like the nearby Jewish kingdom. Indeed there would appear to have been no great rivalry between the groups of priests, and the royal house was apparently very stable. The Nabatean state was democratic, something fairly unusual for the time. It is known that women could accede to the throne, because the names of some queens were passed down, the most famous being Shaquilat, mother of Rabbel II. The wives of the sovereigns bore the title of queen and must have enjoyed

third century BC and with them came the first rock monuments. An age-old controversy surrounds the true function of the structures aligned along the rock walls around the urban center, but it has now been ascertained that many were dwellings, often consisting of a large central hall and a number of smaller rooms set around this. Judging by the few examples of wall decoration that have survived, the rooms were adorned with frescoes in geometrical

considerable status, such to appear beside their consorts on numerous coins. Women were respected in Nabatean society and played an active role, as is confirmed by some funerary inscriptions inferring that they could own their own land, assets and employees. Merchants were at the top of the social pyramid, but sculptors, artists and craftsmen were also afforded some prestige and many artisans passed their trade on from father to son. Civil life was governed by laws and administered by legislators and magistrates.

As far as religion is concerned, the Nabateans venerated non-anthropomorphic gods and, hence, theirs was an aniconical culture; only in the first century AD, contact with the western world brought them to adopt figurative representations of their deities. The most important god was Dusares, who lived on the mountains and controlled natural phenomena; he governed the cycles of the seasons and fertility and was also the protector of the royal house. Later he was assimilated with Dionysus and Jupiter. Al Uzza was the mighty goddess, ruling on matters of life and love and, for this reason, later identified with Aphrodite-Venus. The Nabateans took the cult of the goddess Isis from the Egyptian pantheon.

ARCHITECTURAL MODELS

18 below An Assyrian façade – the style seen in more than half the tombs in Petra. The front is surmounted by one or two bands of crow-steps; in the latter case an undecorated attic level was added between them. Crow steps always include four steps on each side. Originally all the rock tombs in Petra must have had a walled entrance, covered with a layer of plaster inscribed with the name of the deceased. In some cases the plaster may have been replaced with a slab of carved stone. No example of this type of closure has survived here, but it has been seen in the Nabatean necropolis of Hegra, in what is today Saudi Arabia.

The 19th of May, 363 AD marked the beginning of the end for Petra, when an earthquake razed part of the city, seriously damaging many buildings and bringing about the gradual de-population of the city. After the urban fabric shrunk, due to a number of factors, principally the loss of control of trade between the Medi-terranean and the East, a second ring of walls was erected inside the older one and several areas were left in a state of ruin. More earthquakes struck Petra in the following centuries and it was no longer able to recover. When the Crusaders arrived in or around 1116, the superb Nabatean capital had already been reduced to a jumbled mass of ruins. This makes it very difficult to imagine what the Rose-red City looked like and, above all, to believe that the entire valley was once filled with a dense network of roads overlooked by a myriad of white-plastered houses, one or two stories high, each arranged around an inner courtyard full of greenery. As a whole, they must have resembled most of the old flat-roofed dwellings that form the nucleus of many villages in Jordan. At the height of its prosperity, not long after being annexed

by the Roman Empire, Petra looked splendid. At that time, the paved main road, which started near a monumental fountain, ran alongside the bed of Wadi Mousa. On this elegant thoroughfare, flanked on both sides by a continuous colonnade, stood three large markets set on sloping terraces, lined with shops, two temples, palaces and sumptuous public buildings. On the other side of a majestic three-vaulted arch lay a vast sacred precinct, which culminated in an open-air altar and a relatively well-preserved temple, Kasr el Bint. At the mouth of the Siq gorge, the main route into the city, a large theater showed newcomers that the Nabatean kingdom also appreciated the tragedies of Aeschylus, Sophocles and Euripides, and the comedies of Aristophanes. Places of worship were located on the top of the surrounding peaks, as were

18 above A cavetto façade. The cornice that surmounts the lower attic is very similar to the crowning used on pillars in Egyptian temples. A band of multiple crow steps would, of course, have looked totally out of proportion and so two monumental crow steps were invented and also used in the more elaborate double cornice tombs.

19 This is a double-cornice tomb. Numerous variations were developed on this theme, some comprising various architectural elements such as pedimented doorways, taken from the Hellenized western world.

the outposts that formed part of an efficient defensive system. In many ways therefore, Petra resembled the great cities that were, in those years, the pride of Asia Minor and Palestine – Ephesus, Side, Caesarea – but it was also very different. Able merchants and great travellers, the Nabateans were like sponges that had absorbed new ideas from all the peoples they had come into contact with. Being of nomadic origin, and hence lacking building and decorative traditions of their own, they had adopted the figurative languages of others and come up with a highly distinctive art, which freely combined Syrian, Egyptian, Hellenistic and eventually Roman elements. Majestic religious buildings were erected in the center of Petra, similar to the classical temples, but clearly different in certain constructional respects from their models. Kasr al Bint, with its unusual square plan and three adjacent cella, reflects the essential independence that the local builders always managed to maintain with regard to the classical canons. Hundreds of still well-preserved rock faces prove this constructional heterodoxy and not just for their massive use of the so-called "Nabatean capital" (or "horn" capital), a local invention. You have only to observe the Palace Tomb to realize that the proportion of the "golden section" between the various parts – common to

the Greek and Roman worlds – was totally disregarded. Petra is, therefore, unique and, unfortunately, has until now only been studied in part; it holds many surprises.

As almost nothing remains of the city of the living, the attention of visitors is focused on the "city of the dead," the splendid tombs that the Nabateans dug in the sandstone cliffs, sometimes 1,000 feet high or more. This attention is fully justified because it was indeed the rock architecture that made the Nabatean capital famous in ancient times. Scattered over an area of 350 square miles and linked by a dense network of paths and steps cut in the stone, Petra has more than 800 known tombs, temples and dwellings. Some of these structures are extraordinary works, even in comparison with the masterpieces created by the Greeks and

Romans in the same period. The building types are very different and many believe each one to be the expression of a different cultural influence, and of a different period in history. On the other hand, some scholars hold that the various types of façade do not correspond to a precise chronological sequence and that the simple forms continued to be used at the same time as the more elaborate ones. For the sake of convenience, however, the various Nabatean architectural styles are usually divided according to the following classifications.

The first graves used by the Nabateans – which can be dated to the fourth and third centuries BC – were the "ditch graves", usually rectangular, dug in the stone and seen virtually everywhere. The "pit tombs" are thought to be from a slightly later date and are subterranean funerary chambers reached along a sort of conduit; the bodies of the dead were laid inside graves closed with slabs. Very similar to these are the "dromos tombs" (or "rectilinear tombs"); in this case the pit is replaced by a horizontal passageway, the façade is smooth and the door framed with simple pilaster strips or the mere suggestion of an entablature. Far more complex funerary monuments made an appearance in the second century BC, and were known as "Assyrian tombs." The first of these

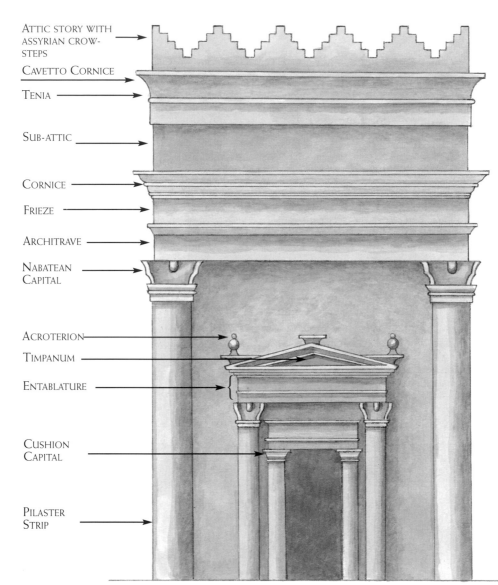

ATTIC STORY WITH ASSYRIAN CROW-STEPS

CAVETTO CORNICE

TENIA

SUB-ATTIC

CORNICE

FRIEZE

ARCHITRAVE

NABATEAN CAPITAL

ACROTERION

TIMPANUM

ENTABLATURE

CUSHION CAPITAL

PILASTER STRIP

20 left This drawing of an imaginary double-cornice façade shows the names of all the various architectural elements. Actually there is only one double-cornice tomb in Petra topped with Assyrian crow-steps. All the others have the standard monumental ones.

20 below The Khasneh is the most striking example of the influence exercised by the Hellenistic culture on Nabatean architecture. It presents all the typical features of the formal language seen in the Greek West: the broken pediment, Corinthian capitals, frieze decorated with festoons and, above all, a massive use of bas-relief statues, totally alien to the local aniconical culture.

20 bottom left The Deir, of which this is a detail, is one of the most remarkable monuments in Petra. Although, like the Khasneh, usually classified as an example of Nabatean Classical style, it greatly differs from it in the somber expressive language adopted, which seems an attempt to break away from Hellenistic influence and formalize an independent Nabatean style which, however, never developed any further.

probably had a very simple, smooth façade crowned with a single band of "crow-steps," below which opened a door, sometimes framed with half-columns; this type of tomb was a typically Nabatean adaptation of models common in nearby Syria. Later, a second band of crow-steps was added above the first.

More sophisticated models developed over the next two centuries, embracing Egyptian influences. In the meantime a particular type had been elaborated, called the "Nabatean capital." The result of this evolution was the **"cavetto tomb,"** with a façade surmounted by a large curved cornice similar to "Egyptian molding," above which are just two monumental crow-steps (these are also called "stepped

tombs"). The front is often enclosed between pilaster strips with Nabatean capitals and the door crowned with entablatures of varying complexity. An elegant transformation of the previous type is the **"double cornice tomb,"** in which an additional classical cornice is introduced below the cavetto cornice. The attic between the two cornices may be filled with short pilaster strips with Nabatean capitals, and the façade is usually marked with two or four pilaster strips that frame an elaborate doorway, often topped with a pediment with tympanum and acroterions.

In the second half of the first century BC Petra adopted architectural motifs from the Hellenized west on a wide scale (such as the Doric frieze and the floral-Corinthian capital), probably

and exemplified by the Roman Soldier Tomb or the Wadi al Najr Tomb, are in **"Roman Classical style,"** subsequent to 106 AD.

The rock structures of Petra may seem to be the product of an incredible waste of energy but in many ways it is less demanding to dig a chamber in the sandstone than to erect a similar structure because the walls and ceilings stand up by themselves. Observation of the Unfinished Tomb has revealed that the digging proceeded from the top downwards. After constructing a wooden scaffolding, the workers first squared and smoothed the rock face with hammers, chisels and saws. Once the funerary chamber had been dug,

the external surface was divided into squares with plumb-lines and cords and the general outline of the various architectural divisions was marked. When all the parts in relief had been completed, the most important façades were probably given a thick layer of plaster as the fragile sandstone did not permit the execution of minute decorative detail. A projecting element in wood was inserted in special grooves to support the plaster (especially over the doors, where the molding was very thick).

The plaster was very possibly painted in bright colors, which must have given the façades a very different appearance from that of today.

introduced by artists from Alexandria. The splendid Khasneh belongs to this phase and was the first example of **"Nabatean Classical style."** From this point on, there was increasingly widespread use of structural elements for ornamental purposes, frequently placed one on top of the other, with chaotic results.

The provincial nature of Nabatean art, developed in a region fairly distant from the Mediterranean basin, in the middle of the desert, justified the continued use of native and obsolete elements of decoration, such as rosettes and contrarampant animals. After the middle of the first century AD, the extremely rich architectural figurative repertoire was joined by an unmistakable desire for scenic grandeur, and the rock façades reached colossal proportions, with orders of columns placed one above the other, imitating temple façades and theatrical backdrops. The Corinthian and Palace Tombs date from this period, while the Deir seems the fruit of an isolated attempt to assert the accomplished independence of Nabatean style from the Hellenistic formal language. Some pediment tombs, resembling the façade of a temple

OBLIVION AND REDISCOVERY

After 1189 – the year in which Saladin conquered Li Vaux Moise, the last crusader outpost to surrender to the Muslim armies – Petra was abandoned and memory of it was lost in the West.

Only a few scholars knew of the phantom city hewn into the rock, described by some Latin, Greek, Byzantine and Arab writers with a disheartening poverty of detail. The oblivion lasted longer than 600 years, until 1812, when the Rose-red City was rediscovered by a young Swiss explorer and Orientalist.

Born in Lausanne in 1784, Johann Ludwig Burckhardt is a fine example of that generation of heroic travellers who were half-scholar, half-adventurer. He helped to redesign geographical maps and knowledge in the early decades of the 19th century.

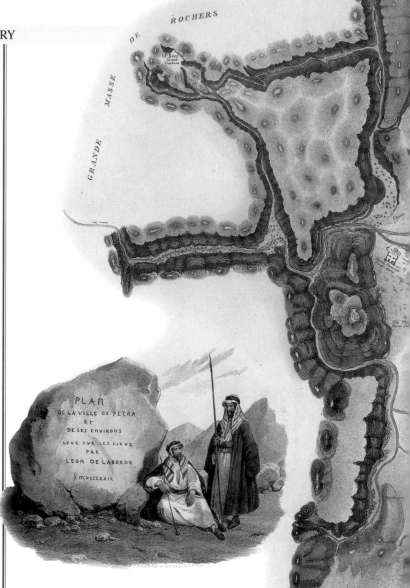

Having joined the Association for Promoting the Discovery of the Interior Parts of Africa, based in London and at least partially controlled by the British Foreign Office, he was officially asked to organize an expedition to Timbuktu in search of the source of the Niger; the British Foreign Office, however, was more interested in obtaining information on the political and economic situation and on transit routes across the Arabian Peninsula. So it was that Burckhardt was sent "undercover" to Cambridge to learn Arabic, as well as a little medicine and astronomy, the latter being essential if he was to trace a map of the region. The young Swiss man was so zealous in his preparation that – as well as sleeping on the ground and walking barefoot – he even had himself circumcised. Within a few years, spent travelling to Malta, Syria and Palestine, the metamorphosis was complete: Burckhardt had become Sheikh Ibrahim Ibn Abdallah, a pious scholar of the Koran and Islamic Law. Those who inquired about his strange accent were told he came from India, upon which he would break into the guttural Swiss-German that he passed off as his Hindustani mother tongue. No one ever doubted him. In the early months of 1812 he was in Amman and a few weeks later arrived at Shawbak, where the ruins of a crusader castle stand; here he was told of a "lost city,"

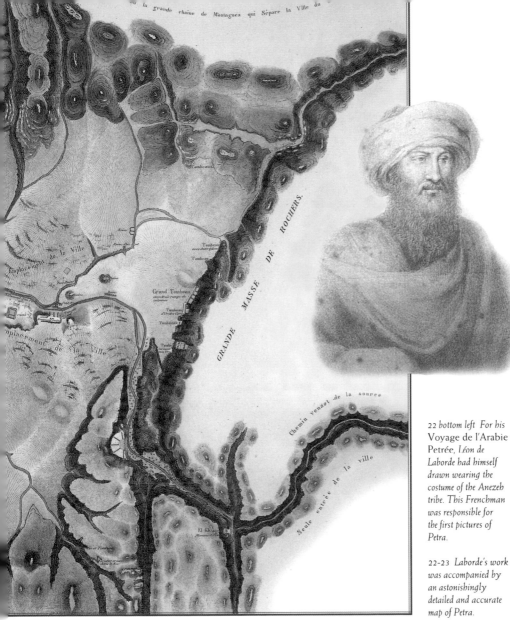

23 top So convincing was Johann Ludwig Burckhardt, the Swiss explorer and Orientalist who discovered Petra in 1812, in his disguise as an Arab scholar that when he died in Cairo in 1817 he was buried according to the Islamic rite with the pseudonym of Ibrahim ibn Abdallah. The written account of his adventure in the Rock City was published posthumously, in 1829, entitled Travels in Arabia, although news of his discovery had spread long before this.

22 bottom left For his Voyage de l'Arabie Petrée, Léon de Laborde had himself drawn wearing the costume of the Anezeh tribe. This Frenchman was responsible for the first pictures of Petra.

22-23 Laborde's work was accompanied by an astonishingly detailed and accurate map of Petra.

23 bottom This view of the ruins of the three-vault arch situated on Colonnade Street is taken from Léon de Laborde's Voyage de l'Arabie Petrée. The author described the monument as "decadent and weighed down with second-rate decorations". The temple known as Kasr el Bint is visible in the background.

inhabited by extremely belligerent Bedouin tribes, not very far away. Knowing that the tomb of Aaron was on the top of Mount Hor, in the immediate vicinity of the mysterious city, Burckhardt expressed the desire to sacrifice a goat on the tomb of the venerated prophet and enlisted the help of a guide. The ruse worked and, although he had to pass in front of the amazing rock monuments without betraying the least emotion to avoid arousing suspicion, he knew he had found the fabulous Petra.

Burckhardt did not have time to thoroughly inspect the ruins but the Bedouins' secret had been exposed. From that moment on, numerous westerners set off for Petra in search

24-25 Laborde and Linant were the first westerners to see the Deir with their own eyes. Burckhardt had not even imagined its existence and Irby and Mangles had been able only to observe it from a distance through a telescope. Although Laborde was not overly enthusiastic about the proportions and style of the building, he was greatly impressed by its size, writing: "Carved in relief out of the rock, it is a compact mass, like a monolithic monument of huge proportions, a gigantic ornament set on the front of the mountain."

24 bottom This picture by Laborde is the first reliable survey made of the Khasneh. The result is truly remarkable as the artist lacked the proper measuring instruments needed to gauge the actual height of the construction. Laborde said that the reproduction of the decorations, friezes and group statues had not been too difficult as the monument was well preserved and very few details had been lost. The ornamentation must have been in better condition than it is today.

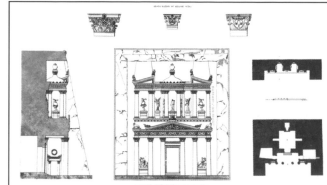

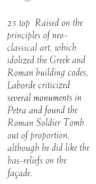

of adventure and improbably dressed in Turkish attire, in a pathetic attempt to pass unnoticed. What actually protected them were the "firmans" received in exchange for a generous reward from the various sheikhs who governed the region. Such xenophobia and hostile mistrust were justified by the long isolation in which the local tribes had lived, the fear of losing centuries-old privileges over passage through the dead city and, above all, by the conviction that the ruins concealed fabulous and as yet undiscovered treasures.

In 1818, just six years after Burckhardt's bold adventure, two British Royal Navy officers arrived in Petra; Charles Irby and James Mangles were accompanied by the painter William Bankes and travelled under the protection of a firman issued by the Sultan of Constantinople, whose jurisdiction included the region of Petra. Irby and Mangles left a vivid written account of their visit; in particular, they were bowled over by the sight of the Khasneh, stating that they did not know what to compare the monument with and that it should probably be considered a unique work.

The first reliable pictures of Petra were by the French Marquis Léon de Laborde and his travelling companion Louis Linant de Bellefonds.

The two reached the Nabatean city in 1828, after having met in Cairo and deciding to embark together on an adventurous expedition to the city discovered 16 years earlier.

Laborde, who was the son of a French diplomat and had considerable financial resources, was then just 19 years old. Bellefonds, son of a Breton naval officer, was 10 years older and already had an excellent reputation as an explorer, engraver, cartographer and expert on the Arab language and

customs. He had spent ten years travelling through Turkey, Syria, Palestine, Egypt, the Libyan Desert and Sudan, studying the local geography and drawing maps.

The two men's stay in Petra lasted a week and was marked by an unusual calm, for the simple fact that the local tribes had been decimated just a few weeks earlier by an outbreak of the plague. Despite the risks, the two decided to take advantage of the unusual situation and carefully drew all the main monuments around them; they also surveyed the interiors of several tombs. After their visit to the Rock City, Linant and Laborde headed for Aqaba where they took the caravan trail to Egypt.

On April 20th 1826 they

25 top Raised on the principles of neo-classical art, which idolized the Greek and Roman building codes, Laborde criticized several monuments in Petra and found the Roman Soldier Tomb out of proportion, although he did like the bas-reliefs on the façade.

25 bottom Laborde was far more enthusiastic about the "gracious form" of the Khasneh, which he defined as "the mark of the might and genius" of the ancient people of Petra.

26 top In line with current opinion, Laborde deemed the so-called Corinthian Tomb a "bad imitation of the Khasneh" although, despite being so bizarre, out of proportion and overloaded with broken lines, it could not be considered totally without grace. Almost as if to temper his judgement, the Frenchman then dwelled on the monument's crumbling appearance, eroded by water and almost suffocated by brambles, lamenting its condition and reflecting on the wretched fate of man's works.

26-27 Laborde admired the huge effort that was needed to dig the theater auditorium out of the cliff and the remarkable condition of the ancient seats. However, its unusual position, in the middle of a necropolis, touched his inner romanticism and he wrote: "What a strange attitude of the spirit is that of a people so accustomed to the idea of death as to become insensitive to it."

separated, as Linant had urgent business to do in Cairo and his companion wanted to stay longer in the Sinai desert.

Back home, Laborde – who would later become keeper of antiquities at the Louvre and then General Manager of the Archives of France – gave the press a report of the expedition, as well as dozens of lithographs based on drawings made by himself and by de Bellefonds. Published in 1830, *Voyage de l'Arabie Petrée* marked the beginning of Levant's knowledge of science and, in particular, of Petra.

Although drawn with what would today be called vaguely naïve taste, the views represented an exhaustive record of Nabatean architecture and the copious notes that accompanied the pictures were filled with detailed observations. Indeed, Laborde was the

first to see the close link between many of Petra's façades and Egyptian and Assyrian monuments. By observing the obvious Hellenistic-Roman influence visible in other buildings, he underlined the derivation of local art.

Similarly, he was the first to describe the so-called "Unfinished Tomb," having guessed its importance from an understanding of the methods used by the ancient builders for these rock constructions, working from the top downwards. His book also contained an extremely detailed and accurate map of the site, used by numerous other travellers in subsequent years.

Laborde's notable work fascinated

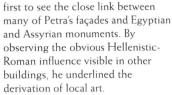

Bellefonds, who gave him an exciting narrative of his experience and offered much generous advice.

In February 1836, after numerous adventures, Stephens at last reached "the Rose-red City, half as old as time," as it was later described by the poet John William Burgon. On his return to America, Stephens had his exciting travel journal printed. His *Incidents of Travel in Egypt, Arabia, Petraea, and the Holy Land* was a bestseller, and made the name of Petra known to the public at large, inspiring generations of readers on both sides of the Atlantic to dream of it.

Three years later, David Roberts also gained permission to camp at

27 right In his comment to this picture, Laborde expressed his regret at not having entered Petra through the Siq, but from the west, and having thus missed the thrill of the sudden and unexpected sight of what are today known as the Royal Tombs. Astonished by the scenographic effect of these colossal carved backdrops, he paused to consider the massive efforts required to construct the Urn Tomb, the first from the right, literally hewn into the cliffside.

a young American lawyer who was travelling across Europe: John Lloyd Stephens, later to become famous for having "discovered" the Maya civilization together with Frederick Catherwood.

In 1835 he was in Paris and happened to come across a copy of *Voyage*. The pictures of the fabulous Petra immediately captured his attention. After postponing his return home, the young American set off for Egypt, from where he intended to travel on to his destination through Sinai. In Cairo he was fortunate enough to meet Louis Linant de

Petra to study the monuments and he brought back exhaustive graphic documentation. Scottish and born in quite a modest social context, Roberts made up for his humble origins by becoming one of the most acclaimed artists of the time. After repeated trips to Europe, in 1838 he set off for Egypt and in the early months of the following year visited the Sinai peninsula, Palestine, Jerusalem, the coasts of Lebanon and Baalbeck.

The lithographs made from the drawings of that extraordinary journey, published in London between 1842 and 1849, brought him

fame that has lasted to the present day. Although a mere 14 in number, his views of Petra are some of the loveliest ever made by an artist; moreover, unlike Laborde's illustrations, the proportions are very accurate, with great attention to detail. It should be said that, unlike his predecessors, Roberts had the aid of a camera lucida, an instrument invented just a few years earlier by William Wollaston and already quite popular. This simple piece of apparatus used a glass prism to superimpose the outline of an object on a sheet of paper and this could then be traced; drawings thus obtained were true to reality.

Fortunately, this enterprising artist and traveller did not merely draw what he saw; he wrote his impressions down in a diary and carefully recorded a great deal of practical information

28 top This picture of David Roberts in Oriental dress was drawn in 1840 by Robert Scott Launder. The garments, sword and belt were among the souvenirs that the famous Scottish painter picked up on his long travels through Egypt and the Holy Land. Roberts remained in Petra from March 6th to the 11th, 1839.

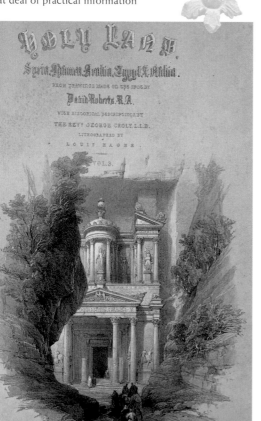

28 bottom Home again in July 1839, Roberts set out to find a publisher. Only after a long search did he find in Francis Graham Moon sufficient interest in his ambitious project. In order to finance the printing of the monumental work, private subscribers were sought which would receive the luxury edition of the lithographs, in large format and hand colored. From 1842 to 1849, using sketches he made in Petra and aided by his formidable memory, Roberts produced the drawings that the Belgian lithographer Louis Haghe gradually turned into prints, published on a monthly basis. The Holy Land, Syria, Idumea, Arabia, Egypt and Nubia eventually comprised six volumes in folio, with 247 plates, including the six frontispieces; that of the third volume was based on the splendid façade of the Khasneh.

29 right This picture by Roberts depicts the auditorium of the great theatre, dug entirely in the rock. Enlarged after the Roman conquest, the building could accommodate approximately 6,000 spectators but its raised stage collapsed after an earthquake and today only a few well-restored parts remain. *Visible in the background, to the left, is the entrance to the Siq; to the right opens the valley and path leading to the High Place of Sacrifice.*

on the places he visited. Today, more than 150 years later, there is still a thrill in reading the description of his adventures.

Roberts reached Petra on the 6th of March 1839 and, thanks to the good services of his local guides and the payment of a conspicuous sum of money, he was allowed to stay for five days on what was the territory of a still quite belligerent tribe. The sight that greeted him was breathtaking and the Scottish artist could not conceal his excitement before such a wonder: "I am increasingly astounded and disconcerted by this extraordinary city...; every ravine has been inhabited, even the mountain tops. The valley is dotted with temples, public buildings, triumphal arches and bridges, each of which has now collapsed, with the exception of one arch and a temple, although its portico has been destroyed. The architectural style is different from anything else I have ever seen and much of it reveals a curious combination of Egyptian, Roman and Greek styles. A stream still flows through the city. Bushes and wild flowers grow lush and prolific; every crack in the rock is filled with them and the air carries the most delicious fragrance." As soon as the camp was organized, Roberts decided to visit the Khasneh, certainly the most famous monument in Petra. He was ecstatic: "... I do not know whether to say I was more surprised by the appearance of the construction or by its remarkable position. It stands, exactly as it was, in a huge recess in the rock and the soft hue of the stone, along with the perfect state of conservation of even tiny details, give the impression that it was only recently completed."

The Siq also caught his attention: "We explored the grand entrance to Petra, which is approximately a mile long and winds between high rocks. These enclose the valley and are so sheer that they seem almost to meet..." This was the spectacular way into the city, still used today by the Bedouins.

Two days after admiring the Khasneh, Roberts wanted to see the other wonder of Petra with his own eyes. Accompanied by a group of armed men, he advanced into a deep

30 top Here Roberts
drew the center of Petra,
where the houses used to
stand. Rising in the
background is the rock
now known as el Habis
and at its foot lie the
ruins of Kasr el Bint,
the great temple that is
the only remaining
fairly well-preserved
raised structure.

gorge along a very rough path which
soon turned into a steep flight of steps;
eventually he came to what is perhaps
the Nabatean city's least visited but
most impressive monuments: "After
proceeding along a rugged gorge and
climbing a crumbling flight of steps for
roughly a mile, we reached a building
called al Deir, or the Monastery,
sculpted in the rock." The Scottish
artist was enthralled by the stunning
spectacle enjoyed from that balcony of
rock extending over the valley below:
"The panorama is superb here, the
gaze sweeps over the valley, Mount

could do was retreat, and Roberts,
after raising camp, continued on
towards Jerusalem: a completely
different picture from the hospitality
that greets the large groups of tourists
who come every day to visit what can
be considered one of the great
archaeological wonders of the world.

After Roberts, an increasing
number of travellers came every year
to the Rose-red City, but the first
official study of its monuments was
not conducted until 1898 by two
German scholars, R. E. Brünnow and
A. Von Domaszewski, who catalogued

30 bottom The remains
of the great three-vault
arch drawn by Roberts
still stand at the eastern
end of the great
Colonnade Street, the
city's main
thoroughfare, on which
stood the markets and
some of the most
important holy
buildings.

Hor – crowned at the top with Aaron's
tomb – and the entire mountain gorge,
which winds among the highest rock
peaks; the ancient city, in all its
breadth stretches out along the
valley."

Unfortunately, despite such
enthusiasm, Roberts' stay in Petra was
marred by minor incidents – including
the theft of some crockery –
culminating on the fifth day in an
attack by marauders who, among
other things, took guns and
ammunition. At that point all they

more than 800 rock structures, giving
each one a number that is still used
today.

Until the end of the First World
War, only German archaeologists
studied the Nabatean City. The British
followed them when the Trans-Jordan
emirate was formed in 1921. In the
meantime the first systematic
reconnaissance of the zone was
conducted and a reliable map of the
urban area drawn up.

The first real excavation
campaigns, this time directed by an

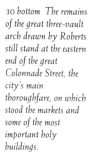

30-31 Roberts was much impressed by the Royal Tombs, which he portrayed from several angles. That shown to the right, known as the Urn Tomb, is certainly one of the most interesting because of the way the façade is set back from the outline of the cliff in a clear attempt to create a scenographic effect. The result is made all the more effective by the perspective line of the two lateral colonnades.

31 bottom While in Petra, Roberts witnessed a dispute between Bedouins and decided to reproduce the scene. One of the men had been accused of theft and the authoritative opinion of three of the tribe's sheikhs was sought to settle the matter. The rock building seen behind the group is the Urn Tomb.

31

32 top Roberts' picture shows the arch that used to span the Siq and marked its entrance. The lower part was cut into the rock and decorated with two deep niches, which presumably contained the statues of protective deities. The arch collapsed in 1896 following a minor earthquake.

32 bottom Visitors approaching the archaeological site of Petra today from the village of Wadi Mousa first encounter some of the most striking rock tombs in the area. These are large monolithic rocks, isolated from the slope of the mountain and now known as Djin or "Spirit" Blocks. A little farther ahead, on

the left, stand two singular rock tombs, one above the other: The upper one is known as the Obelisk Tomb, and the lower one is called the Bab el Siq Triclinium. This veduta is one of the few in which Roberts took some "poetic license," altering the actual arrangement of the monuments portrayed.

English team, date from 1929. Since then, numerous other archaeological missions – including those of Jordan, France and the United States – have succeeded one another in the dual and difficult task of preserving what remains and, above all, discovering what still lies beneath the sands of Petra. Indeed, an extraordinary and illuminating discovery was made in December 1993, in a room adjacent to the Byzantine church. Between 1992

and 1993 this religious building had already caused a great stir when splendid and well-preserved mosaic floors were uncovered. No one, however, imagined that a large number of charred scrolls, extremely fragile but still legible using the proper techniques, would emerge from the debris of the building. A preliminary study has revealed that they are mostly inventories, registers and land records written in Greek. The experts think

that at least 50 of them can be translated in the immediate future and will provide precious information on the economy of fifth- and sixth-century Petra.

Clearly, there is still a lot to be discovered in the city build in the rock.

32-33 On the morning of March 8th 1839, Roberts, escorted by a group of armed men, advanced into a deep gorge along a very rough path which soon turned into a steep flight of steps approximately a mile long. At the end of their climb, the group reached the stunning construction known as al Deir, or the Monastery, the most impressive monument in the Nabatean City and one of the best preserved.

33 bottom Like most modern-day visitors to Petra, Roberts fell under the spell of the Khasneh and decided to immortalize it in three vedutas. The subject of this one is its portico, at the time missing one of its four colossal columns. As well as by the size of the structure, the Scottish artist was struck by the splendid quality of execution of the friezes. It is not therefore surprising that he formulated the opinion that the true function of Petra's rock structures may have been merely to please the refined aesthetic taste of the Nabateans.

33

Petra

34 left The Khasneh
seen from above; this
splendid rock mausoleum
has now become the
symbol of Petra.

34 top right Detail of
one of the semi-pediments
of the Khasneh, with its
festooned friezes and
Corinthian capitals.

34 bottom right A
detail of the tholos on
the Khasneh, showing
the bas-relief statue of
the goddess Tyche - Al
Uzza.

35 Some of the
Assyrian tombs that
line the walls of the
Outer Siq.

THE SIQ, FROM WADI MOUSA TO THE THEATRE

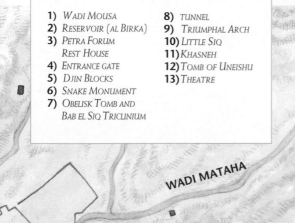

LEGEND

1) WADI MOUSA
2) RESERVOIR (AL BIRKA)
3) PETRA FORUM REST HOUSE
4) ENTRANCE GATE
5) DJIN BLOCKS
6) SNAKE MONUMENT
7) OBELISK TOMB AND BAB EL SIQ TRICLINIUM
8) TUNNEL
9) TRIUMPHAL ARCH
10) LITTLE SIQ
11) KHASNEH
12) TOMB OF UNEISHU
13) THEATRE

WADI MATAHA

WADI MUTHLIM

JEBEL EL KHUBTHA

N

WADI MOUSA

Before commencing a visit to the Rose-red City, a little time should be dedicated to the village of Wadi Mousa (or El Ji); this is visited every year by thousands of tourists but most are unaware that this agglomeration of white houses has a history of its own: one that goes back to the dawn of time, as it probably stands on the site of the ancient Gaia, first an Edomite settlement and then,

36 left In recent years, the government has built numerous houses in Wadi Mousa (seen here from Moghar al Nassara) to accommodate the Bedouins who until recently lived in the tombs of Petra. Some families, however, continue to live on the archaeological site.

in the sixth century BC, the home of the Nabatean kings before the court was moved to Petra. The inhabitants worshipped Dusares, the greatest god in the Nabatean pantheon, not surprisingly also known as the "god of Gaia."

In the upper part of the village is the famous Ain Mousa spring where, according to the Bible (Exodus 17:1-7), Moses struck the rock with his staff and brought forth water to quench the thirst of the people of Israel during their exhausting journey to the Promised Land.
As suggested by the many place-

names that contain the word Mousa (which means *Moses*), the entire region is permeated with the memory of the patriarch's passage. The spring supplies the river known as Wadi Mousa, after which the village is named, and is today protected by a white building that resembles a mosque. This spring made the birth of the Nabatean settlement possible, and it is easy to imagine how sacred it must have been in such an arid region.

Not far away from Wadi Mousa are the excavations of the Edomite settlement of Tawilan.

36-37 The name Wadi Mousa means literally "the Valley of Moses" and the village developed around the spring which the patriarch is supposed to have produced out of the rock to refresh the Jews during the exodus from Egypt. Once a major suburb of Petra, today it has numerous hotels, restaurants and other enterprises, all serving the flourishing tourist industry.

37 bottom right Until a few years ago, the area where the Petra Forum Rest House now stands was occupied by a government hotel that incorporated a fine Nabatean tomb. When the old structure was demolished, the tomb – now a luxurious bar – was restored and returned to the open air; its main attraction is the colonnaded courtyard before it.

37 top *The first Nabatean rock tombs can be seen just a few dozen yards from the village of Wadi Mousa, along the normally arid course of the river; these were part of the necropolis of the ancient Gaia.*

all its force against this and eventually opened a narrow passage – the Siq. Today there is no longer any risk because the flow of the water has been diverted a few meters before the mouth of the gorge, which is protected by a solid embankment. As will be explained later, this is exactly what the Nabateans had themselves already done.

THE TOMB OF PETRA FORUM REST HOUSE

A visit to ancient Petra can commence even before one passes through the entrance to the archaeological site. Indeed, attentive observers will notice some Nabatean tombs dug in the banks of white sandstone around the Visitor's Center. As they are greatly eroded, most of these look more like natural caves, but they are all that remains of the necropolis of Gaia. One monumental tomb is incorporated in the modern Petra Forum Rest House, to the immediate right of the entrance. Clearly visible from the parking lot in front, it has a double-cornice façade, which has lost its battlement; apart from this it is in

THE SIQ

The Siq, a narrow gorge eroded by water and wind over thousands of years, is the most spectacular, easiest and most popular way into the Nabatean capital. It seems incredible that a small trickle of water like Wadi Mousa – which also flows through the village of the same name and runs for a long stretch on the left side of the road between the entrance gate and the mouth of the gorge – could have produced such a phenomenon. Yet, during the rainy season and after the most violent summer storms this

pitiful little stream turns into a howling mass of water and has been responsible for numerous tragedies; in 1967 a flash flood took a group of tourists inside the Siq by surprise and most of them drowned. Observing the conformation of the valley around Wadi Mousa you will see exactly how such violent floods occur: Like a huge funnel, it gathers rainwater from the side valleys and gradually narrows until it reaches a colossal bank of sandstone; for centuries the kinetic energy of the river was discharged in

excellent condition partly because it had been used as a dwelling and stables for centuries. Known as *Al Khan*, it is particularly striking for the imposing colonnade that fronts each side, also carved into the rock. Also in the hotel area are the remains of a large Nabatean reservoir, known as Al Birka, into which some of the water from Ain Mousa must have been channelled. It seems certain that the precious liquid was carried from here, along a long pipe, to Petra, where it supplied the great nymphaeum at the beginning of Colonnade Street. The ruins of several kilns used to bake the characteristic Nabatean pottery have been discovered around the reservoir.

38 *It is easier to assess the amount of work that was needed to make the Djin Blocks from on high; these three structures were created from as many outcrops after a massive feat of excavation. At the top of the highest block, to the left, you will see a rectangular cavity which may have been a loculus. This would confirm the funerary function of these monuments. The sort of slanting plane, excavated in the wall behind and today much eroded, could have been used to hoist the sarcophagus, which was then put in place using a footbridge. Behind the three tower-*

tombs is some of the audacious channelling that formed part of the complex hydraulic system designed by the Nabateans to supply Petra with drinking water. On the left, in the foreground, you will also see the mouths of unusual hypogea, devoid of external decoration, created by hollowing out some natural formations. The chambers thus obtained, probably used as burial places, are thought by some scholars to be among the oldest rock structures in Petra, dating from before the second century BC and therefore even older than the Djin Blocks.

Past the entrance gate, a two-lane dirt road descending to the southeast follows the bed of the river, in recent years controlled for safety reasons. This is Bab al Siq, the Gate to the Siq, the last stretch of the valley eroded by Wadi Mousa in a solid bank of white sandstone that creates a sharp contrast with the reddish hilltops. The scenery is already delightful, the rounded stones pockmarked with holes and cavities produced by the wind, and speckled with numerous shades of pink, salmon and saffron.

distant past, all that now remain are the holes and grooves they were fixed in. Although now they are thought probably to be tower-tombs (among the oldest in Petra), the word *Djin* in Arabic means "spirit" and these could indeed have been created as divine simulacra, containers of guardian spirits placed to protect the entrance

the Djin blocks, which vanishes in the distance at an almost constant gradient; this is what remains of the channel that conveyed the water from Moses' Spring to Petra.

It becomes a constant presence all along the Siq, and a little observation reveals that the mountain sides surrounding the Rose-red City are literally dotted with similar channels; as it has already been said, the Nabateans were exceptional hydraulic engineers.

The valley narrows gradually, enclosed by increasingly high cliffs and suddenly, three mysterious-looking structures appear to the right. These are the so-called Djin Blocks, huge monolithic cubes cut away from the slope behind in a colossal work of excavation. Dating perhaps from the first century BC and between 20 and 30 feet high, they stand solemn and majestic; one supports a pyramidal stepped structure at the top and the sides of another are adorned with four half-columns. The plinths, capitals, architraves and cornices must have been made in marble or bronze and then mounted in the rock. Wrenched away by some plunderer of the

to the Nabatean capital. Others believe that they represent the god Dusares, originally represented by the Nabateans in the form of a cube. However, the three monoliths are also known as *Sahrij*, which in Arabic means *water tank*. This idea may seem strange because these structures are totally unsuited to the function of cistern, but there are 23 similar cubes in Petra and the immediate vicinity, all situated near springs or rivers. The Djin may have been considered the homes or the containers of the spirits that guarded the Nabateans' most precious possession, water. It is interesting to observe a long horizontal cleft in the rock behind

39 *The true purpose of the Djin blocks is not yet certain but, as two of the three blocks in Bab al Siq have an internal*

cavity, they were probably tombs. In other cases, the burial chamber is thought to have been built on top of them.

THE OBELISK TOMB

After the Djin blocks, the right side of Bab al Siq becomes a succession of rock tombs, most of which are Assyrian in type. Water channels and small cisterns dug in the rock can be seen. A few dozen yards farther down, on the left, stands the elaborate architectural elevation of Petra's first, great monumental tomb, which at first glance looks like a single monument. Actually these are two separate tombs, dug one on top of the other in different periods. There was probably a functional link between the two structures, but for the moment this possibility has not been investigated. The upper structure, unique in Petra and known as the Obelisk Tomb, owes its name to the four large pyramid-shaped obelisks that dominate it; approximately 20 feet high and sculpted in full relief out of the rock, these are probably of Egyptian influence. A niche in the wall behind the obelisks contains a standing male statue, dressed in Hellenistic fashion. A door flanked by pillars and surmounted by a Doric frieze leads into the funeral

chamber that contained five graves. The most important, in the back wall, is in the form of an arcosolium. A widely accepted theory holds that each pyramid, called *nefesh*, portrays one of the deceased; if this is so the tomb was probably initially constructed to house four people and a fifth laid here later had himself portrayed in the new fashion, the

arcosolium having been dug for him. If, on the other hand, the obelisks and statues were of the same period, this would demonstrate the continuing use of ancient funeral customs combined with the figurative language imported from the Greco-Roman West. This is only a theory, as other writers believe that the obelisks were actually intended as *mazeboth*, as described in the Bible, i.e. divine simulacra. Their presence at the very mouth of the Siq therefore served to exercise powerful protection over the city. Whatever the correct theory, it is common knowledge that the Obelisk Tomb dates from the first half of the first century AD, and the Triclinium from the second half.

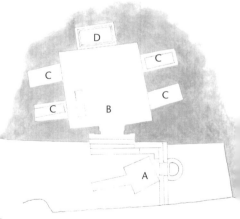

A PIT TOMB
B FUNERARY CHAMBER
C LOCULI
D ARCOSOLIUM
  LOCULUS

A CHAMBER
B TRICLINIAL BED

40 bottom left The four massive obelisks marking its front make this tomb unique in Petra.

THE BAB AL SIQ TRICLINIUM

The monument dug immediately below what has just been described is in far poorer condition, although it is a few decades more recent. It is attributed to the reign of Rabbel II (71-106 AD), the last Nabatean king, or his immediate predecessor, Malchus II. As the name says, this is not a proper tomb, but a room used for the wakes and feasts held to honor the deceased; Petra has numerous other similar places, of clear western influence. The Roman *triclinium* consisted of three adjacent beds or benches arranged around the three sides of a table, and two or three persons lay on each bed; by extension, the term later came to mean the dining room itself. The deceased for whom the monument was built may have been buried in the two graves on the sides of the façade, or even in the Obelisk Tomb above. In stark contrast with the elaborately marked front (very similar to the lower part of the Corinthian Tomb), the interior is extremely bare, save for the great stone *triclinium* that runs around three sides of the simple rectangular chamber. An inscription in two languages, Nabatean and Greek (in reduced form), is visible on one of the rocks that face the two structures. It reads as follows: "This is the funeral site chosen by Abdmank, son of Akayus, son of Shullay, son of Utaih for the construction of a tomb for himself, his heirs and the heirs of his heirs, for eternity and beyond. He did this during his life, in the ... year of the reign of Malchus." Given

the position of the epigraph, many scholars no longer believe it is related to the Obelisk Tomb and think that it pertains to some pit graves situated nearby. Doubts remain and it is also impossible to ascertain which Malchus the inscription refers to; the uncertainty surrounding the date is quite considerable as Malchus I reigned from 59 to 30 BC and Malchus II was king from 40 to 70 AD. The use of Greek, moreover, shows that, between the first century BC and the first century AD, Petra had become a cosmopolitan city.

An unusual burial place lies a short distance before the two tombs, again on the left of Bab al Siq; this is known as the Snake Tomb because of a very worn bas-relief, the interpretation of which is still dubious.

A path that is extremely rugged and at times rather difficult to see starts from the Triclinium Tomb and leads through what looks almost like a moonscape to El Madras, once one of Petra's suburbs. From this area, dotted with rock structures, you can choose to continue to the northwest and return to the Siq later along an extraordinary number of flights of steps cut in the rock, directly to the left of the Khasneh. This is a tiring route suited to expert hikers and is tackled by the adventurous few.

40-41 Although the Obelisk Tomb and the triclinium below seem to be one structure, they are actually two separate monuments dating from different periods, as demonstrated by the fact that the two façades are not vertically aligned.

41 top left Although the elements have caused considerable damage to the façade of the Bab al Siq Triclinium, it is still readable and constitutes a fine example of what is known as "Nabatean classical style." It has much in common with the other broken pediment Nabatean tombs and, above all, with the Corinthian Tomb.

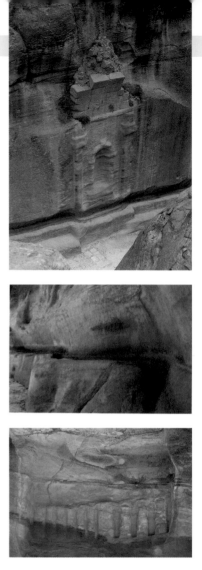

Continuing down along the dirt track, after no more than 300 yards it suddenly turns left into the proper Siq or Interior Siq. Before entering this spectacular gorge, you should stop a moment to observe a few details. First of all, you will see that a huge dam, reconstructed in 1963 and again in 1991 bars the mouth of the Siq, and that the course of Wadi Mousa has been diverted to the right, towards a tunnel. The modern road crosses the riverbed on a bridge, also recently constructed, and starts to descend in

the narrow fissure. This is a fairly true reconstruction of what the Nabateans did to control Wadi Mousa between the first century BC and the beginning of the first century AD. This is when the bottom of the Siq was paved with stone and, to prevent the disastrous winter floods, Wadi Mousa was conveyed into a deep channel dug into the rock; a tunnel (280 feet long and known as *al Muthlim*) was built to carry the waters to a side valley. In this way Wadi Mousa – first along Wadi Muthlim, then along Wadi Mataha – is forced to circumnavigate the mountain of El Khubtha before returning to its ancient bed in the

Petra valley, at the beginning of Colonnade Street. This is a brilliant and extremely complicated work of hydraulic engineering. Moreover, in order for the canal from Bab al Siq to enter the Siq and continue on towards the city, it had to cross the river. It probably did so in conduits in the bridge that was used by caravans on their way to Petra. Near the tunnel, to the right, a Djin block confirms the link between this type of monument and places of flowing water. Once past the tunnel there are interesting monuments to visit, described under the Little Siq. The entrance to the Siq is marked by the remains of a monumental arch, of which only the two abutments cut into the rock face and decorated with two niches (which must have housed votive statues) and some hewn stones of the arch itself have survived. This daring construction – a sort of triumphal arch, or perhaps a form of defense with heavy wooden doors – collapsed in 1896 following an earthquake, but its appearance is known thanks to some lithographs by David Roberts and other contemporary artists. The monument reveals Greco-Roman influence and dates from the latter half of the first century AD. The two fissures visible in the walls that enclose the passage are the channels that carried water from Moses' Spring to the city; the water flowed at first in the open air before being forced through cylindrical clay pipes, lodged in the rock channel with plenty of mortar. Some sections of this piping, very similar to its modern equivalent, are on display in the New Museum. Large sections of the aqueduct were exposed and restored during excavation work conducted along the Siq between 1997 and 1998. At the same time tons of gravel and sand that had accumulated after the floods provoked by the collapse of the Nabatean dam were removed and large sections of the original flooring were discovered. This paving, most of which was considered lost, probably dates from the first century AD, but may even go back to the Roman conquest; this suggestion is supported by the fact that the *Via Nova Traiana* –

a straight road to Aqaba – had already been completed and the Siq had become the main way into Petra.

The Interior Siq is a spectacular natural fault – produced perhaps by tectonic forces and then worn smooth by the waters of Wadi Mousa – approximately one mile long. Of a mysterious and disquieting charm, it is a very narrow (in some points no more than 10 feet wide) winding passage, perpetually steeped in shadow and enclosed between 300-to 600-foot high walls that at certain points seem to touch and block out the sky. At intervals they suddenly separate to form natural projecting roofs. These areas were used as caravanserai by caravans arriving in Petra. Along both walls of the fissure are a number of votive niches and stelae, which suggest that the Siq was sacred not only for the Nabatean people, as numerous

42 top left and top right All that remains of the great monumental arch that marked the entrance to the Siq are the abutments carved in the rock and adorned with pilaster strips and niches.

42 center right Two aqueducts are dug into the rock on both sides of the Siq.

42 bottom right More than 50 votive niches containing baetyli (up to 10, as in this picture) have been found along the Siq. Sometimes accompanied by inscriptions, they are probably manifestations of religious beliefs left by Nabatean merchants on their way to and from Petra.

43 left This niche, dug in the Siq, contains an egg-shaped baetylus and has a dedication in Greek to the god Dusares that dates from the second century AD.

43 right This quite elaborate religious niche in the Siq is one of many carved in the form of an aedicula with pilaster strips and a pediment.

feet and the legs of the two men. The figures are almost twice lifesize, and it is easy to imagine the thrill this unexpected vision must have stirred in those arriving in Petra for the first time.

The Khasneh appears farther on, at a point where the Siq veers to the right. This rock monument is unequalled anywhere else in the world and however well-prepared you may think you are for the spectacle, its sudden appearance – a remarkable contrast between the delicately pink façade and the dark gloomy Siq – will take your breath away. With its totally symmetric front and exquisite proportions, the Khasneh is certainly one of the wonders of antiquity.

44 bottom left The Siq is a spectacular fissure created by tectonic motion and then worn smooth by the waters of Wadi Mousa. So close are the walls that in many parts they block out the view of the sky.

44 center top Halfway along the Siq is an outcrop of sandstone, with a large votive aedicula on one side, containing two baetyli, one adorned with a stylized face.

44 center bottom Along the Siq there are also some underground chambers, the function of which has not yet been clarified. The possibility that they were tombs has been

excluded but it also seems difficult to believe that they were dwellings. More probably they housed the guards that defended the main entrance to Petra.

inscriptions date from the second and third centuries AD. Many niches contain just one *baetylus*, but some have several, up to a maximum of 10. Halfway along, where the passage widens considerably, stands a solitary sandstone block shaded by a single wild fig tree. The side facing those leaving Petra has a large niche framed by two pillars with Nabatean capitals, surmounted by an elegant architrave with a Doric frieze. Inside, side by side, are two *baetyli*; the smaller right-hand one is smooth, whereas that on the left features a highly stylized face with square eyes and a straight nose. This niche, the largest known in the Siq, dates from the reign of Malchus II (40-70 AD). Not far ahead, on the left-hand wall, is a remarkable group of statues uncovered in 1998 when digging was conducted to lower the road by more than six feet. Although the whole upper part is greatly eroded, it is still possible to recognize the figures of two merchants each leading two dromedaries. The animals' feet are still perfectly distinguishable, as are the *caligae*-clad

44-45 and 44 bottom right A group of statues portraying a caravan was found in the spring of 1998 in the Siq. Unfortunately, as no one could have known it was there, the hooves of the animals were broken during excavation work by the bucket of a digger. The pieces will shortly be returned to their original place.

45 The sudden sight of the Khasneh as you enter Petra from the deep fissure of the Siq is a unique experience. So much perfection seems truly of another world.

The Khasneh

Without doubt Petra's most famous monument, the Khasneh is also the best preserved thanks to a protected position that has saved it from the elements. This amazing structure is carved deep into a sheer rock face at the point where the Siq makes an unexpected and sharp right turn. The best time to admire the Khasneh is between 8:45 and 10:15 am, when the rock takes on the most fantastic colors. The proportions are formidable. The façade, 130 feet high and 92 feet wide, is divided into two stories, the lower one consisting of a portico with a pediment and six

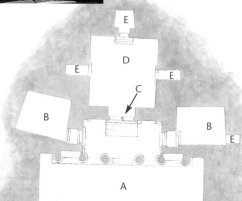

46 top The delicate ornaments carved in fragile sandstone to embellish the façade of the Khasneh are an eloquent demonstration of the skill acquired by the Nabatean artists.

A VESTIBULE
B SIDE ROOMS
C PURIFYING BASIN
D GREAT HALL
E NICHES (OR LOCULI)

46-47 The Khasneh is fronted by an open space scattered with alluvium. Recent surveys have shown that the ancient paving of this area lies at a depth of more than 13 feet. The monument was therefore probably originally reached from a high flight of steps.

46 bottom The intercolumns of the upper floor contain carved bas-reliefs of female figures. Six of them, although extremely worn, can be identified as amazons thanks to their short tunics and axes brandished above their heads. In the past, however, they were thought to be Maenads.

47 top left The external intercolumns of the vestibule contain relief figures of the Dioscuri.

47 top right The roof of the tholos is sumptuously adorned with a crown of frontal palmette tiles.

Corinthian columns 40 feet high. Despite appearances, only the two central columns are free-standing, the other four being connected to the mass behind. Two huge equestrian groups carved in high relief between the external pairs very probably represent the Dioscuri. These sculptures are very worn as are the other nine relief figures that adorn the façade, but the damage is only partially ascribable to natural erosion, the main culprits being Christian and Muslim iconoclasts; careful observation reveals holes left on and around the figures by rifle shots. The design of the frieze running above the

columns consists of foliage and volutes alternating with vases framed by facing griffins; a scroll decoration completes the *tympanum*, which had at the center a Gorgon's head (interpreted by some writers as an eagle with outspread wings). In the corners of the architrave two lions (or sphinxes) have the function of acroteria. The upper part of the attic that separates the two stories presents an unbroken row of rosettes.
The second story, of aerial elegance, is divided into three parts. At the center is a *tholos*, or round templet, with a conical roof topped by an urn. This is what gave the building its Arab name,

47 center The tympanum of the pediment is decorated with a much-ruined figure, interpreted as the bust of a Gorgon emerging from a background of foliage.

47 bottom The monument's full Arab name, Khasneh al Faraoun (the Pharaoh's Treasury), is based on a legend totally devoid of historical foundation.

the Treasury; the Bedouins believed that it contained immense riches and, in an attempt to gain possession of these, repeatedly fired their rifles at it, with the intention of smashing it. The *tholos* is flanked by two semi-pediments, each one supported by corner columns; the two niches to the rear, set against the back wall, stand between two pairs of paired semicolumns. The four figures adorning the semi-pediments and the two at the sides of the *tholos* are identifiable as amazons brandishing axes in their right hands. The two sculptures in the two rear niches represent winged Nikes. Far more problematic was the interpretation of the female figure in the central intercolumn of the *tholos*.

The figure is holding a cornucopia in her left hand and a patera in her right, typical of the goddess Tyche (Destiny, but here meaning Fortune); moreover, slightly below, the acroterion around the apex of the pediment is in a solar disk set between ears of wheat and framed by another two cornucopias. Such symbology is closely related to the goddess Isis. On this basis there is a tendency today to see her as the goddess Isis assimilated with Tyche and at the same time the Nabatean goddess Al Uzza, in accordance with a form of syncretism widely recorded in Hellenistic times. This identification is supported by a comparison of the way the goddess is posed with similar portrayals of Tyche-Isis on vases of Alexandrian production, in particular a Ptolemaic jug worked in relief and housed in Stuttgart. An unbroken entablature with a frieze depicting garlands of leaves and nuts runs above the capitals of the second story and four huge eagles served as acroteria. The interior of the building – quite disappointing compared with its grand façade – consists of a large vestibule or pronaos, 46 feet wide and 19 deep, with eight steps leading to the central chamber; this is a large cube, 40 feet

square, flanked on three sides by smaller rooms. The only decorations are the pedimented surrounds to the three doors. Another two smaller rooms, also reached via steps, flank the vestibule. The exceptional architectural type seen in the Khasneh, as well as the complex and refined decorations, would suggest the work of craftsmen from afar, probably from Alexandrian cultural circles or at least influenced by Greek artistic style, who worked side by side with the local stone cutters. Equally, it could be a design by a Nabatean artisan trained in Hellenistic spheres. This dilemma is closely related to the age-old debate as to the date of the monument. Today there is a tendency to reject the idea that the Khasneh was erected at the time of the emperor Hadrian's visit to Petra (in 129 or 130), with a more likely date being a period between the middle of the first century BC and the middle of the first century AD. There is also an open debate as to the purpose of the Khasneh: tomb or temple? The arrangement of the

internal rooms and the presence of niches that could quite easily have contained sarcophagi would suggest it was used for burials rather than as a sanctuary. Such a fine monument could only have been the tomb of a king and, considering the date proposed, this monarch may have been Aretas III Philhellen, Obodas II or Aretas IV, responsible for Petra's urban renewal. The matter is so far unresolved.

48 bottom left One of the pillars of the pronaos, the third from the left, collapsed at an unknown time and was restored in 1960.

48 center top The vestibule, 46 feet wide and 20 deep, leads to a large chamber and two small rooms that open on each side of it.

48 center bottom The interior of the Khasneh consists of a large room, 40 feet square with huge doorways leading to three smaller rooms.

48 top right The capitals that adorn the Khasneh are a local interpretation of the classical Corinthian modules, imported from the Greek world.

48 bottom right There is a magnificent view of the narrow mouth of the Interior Siq from inside the large chamber.

49 left You will see a hemispherical hollow on the threshold of the large chamber linked to a second basin via a small channel dug in the rock; this is a purifying bowl which collected the blood of sacrificed goats.

49 right Superb, spectacular and well preserved, the Khasneh has become the symbol of Petra.

50 left Tomb 70, situated on the left side of the Outer Siq, is easily recognized thanks to its singular appearance. Considerably out from the back wall, it is surrounded by a crown of battlements and has three identical sides.

50 top right On the side opposite the façade of the Khasneh, on the right wall of the Siq, is a large opening without a façade. This was presumably a triclinium *and is one of the largest in Petra.*

51 top left High up along the walls of the Outer Siq runs the channel which contained the earthenware pipes of the aqueduct; the water flowed through these at high pressure.

51 bottom left Tomb 67 is one of the group of four adjacent tombs dug in the left-hand wall of the Outer Siq, not far from the Khasneh. Of the "double-cornice" type, it is known for the remarkable funerary chamber on the attic level, between the two crow-stepped battlements. The square-plan chamber is totally bare.

The gorge veers to the right from the clearing on which stands the Khasneh and starts to descend sharply towards the ancient city.

There are tombs on both sides, dug at a certain height from the ground and now in quite bad condition. On the left not far beyond

a large square chamber (which could have been a *triclinium*) opened in the opposite wall, the most attentive observers will see the remains of a façade (number 66 in Brünnow's classification) with a still-preserved circular and diamond-shaped base, surmounted by a right-hand pilaster strip. Part of the structure collapsed in 1847 destroying its Greek epigraph; this, however, had been copied and is known to be the tomb of Arriano, who died at the age of 27 of "an illness that overwhelms all" and was mourned by his elderly mother. Initially still confined between high walls (the course of the aqueduct is easily distinguished on the right, high

above the ground, with several terracotta pipes still in place), the gorge then widens suddenly. For this reason it here takes the name of Outer Siq. The most striking structures include, to the left, a large double-cornice tomb, its portal framed by four high pilaster strips, and the subsequent Tomb 70, the main body, which is crowned with a crow-step battlement and juts out significantly from the rock face. The road now runs beside the normally dry bed of a seasonal river, created by the streams that descend during the winter rains from the side valleys. The inconsistent stream now carries tons of pebbles and sand downstream, but at the height of Petra's splendor – starting from the reign of Aretas IV – the Siq looked very different. First, the road level was six to nine feet lower than now and the road was paved.

The river was robustly channelled and perhaps later even covered; the waters surfaced hundreds of yards downstream and joined those of Wadi Mousa and Wadi Mataha near a *nymphaeum*, described later. To the right and left, dozens of tombs created a backdrop of great scenographic effect. You can imagine the thrill that this sight must have stirred in the merchants arriving in Petra with their caravans from distant lands after crossing boundless deserts. Approximately 200 yards before the theater, the Siq forms a natural arena; on the sides of this – to the left in

52-53 *This view of the hollow that opens along the Outer Siq, shortly before the Theater, clearly highlights the characteristic rows of tombs cut into the rock. To the rear rise the mountains that surround the urban area.*

52 bottom *Standing out amidst the myriad of façades crammed along the mountain walls are some highly elaborate and large tombs, which were the burial places of Petra's richest families.*

particular – are aligned dozens of tombs in several rows. Most are crowned with single and double battlements but several are arched; others are of the cavetto or double-cornice type. These tombs are linked to one another by narrow passages and flights of steps, giving the impression of streets lined with buildings; not surprisingly they are known as the "Streets of Façades." The fact that many of the tombs on the lowest levels seem half-buried by alluvial detritus (such that you can no longer see the entrance to some of them), demonstrates how violently Wadi Mousa returned to the Siq after the collapse of the Nabatean dam built at its mouth.

53 top The ceaseless erosive action of the elements has devastated many of the façades that once adorned the sides of the Siq, though they have now become splendid works of abstract art.

53 center In some parts (such as the valley that opens to the left of the Outer Siq, top), as well as the customary rock tombs, there are quarry faces from which the Nabateans obtained their building materials.

53 bottom This spectacular aerial view of the Outer Siq demonstrates that the rock tombs flank the main valley on terraces at various levels, achieving
spectacular effects. These were originally joined by flights of steps, which earned this particular stretch of the Siq the nickname of "Streets of Façades."

54 top Inside, the tomb of Uneishu is a vast roughly square-shaped chamber, as usual completely bare, with three loculi in the back wall and another four in each of the two side walls. Spacious and dry because of its raised position above the bottom of the Siq, the tomb was long inhabited by the Bedouins. Indeed, until the middle of the 20th century, a similar form of reuse was common among most of the Nabatean necropolises.

THE TOMB OF UNEISHU

54-55 To the extreme right in the picture is the Tomb of Uneishu, not to be confused with a similar tomb that stands not far from it (visible at the center).

55 top The Tomb of Uneishu has a double-cornice façade and the doorway, between pilaster strips with Nabatean capitals, is crowned with an elegant pediment. The monument was preceded by a colonnaded courtyard, onto which opened a triclinium.

55 bottom The rock wall of the Outer Siq near the Tomb of Uneishu contains a large number of rock structures, most with very severe façades, crowned with the typically Assyrian crow-stepped battlements. At the corners there are sometimes pilaster strips with characteristic Nabatean "horn" capitals, and simple pediments of classical inspiration may surmount the entrance doorways. The various burial places were linked by flights of steps and paths, some of which are still usable.

By rights this tomb should be included on the next itinerary, because it is one of the so-called "Royal Tombs;" however, its location suggests inclusion here for the visitor's convenience. It is entered from the road that runs along the bottom of the Siq, by climbing up a path to the right, before the theater. Its majestic double-cornice façade, set slightly back from the edge of the mountain, is very easy to identify. Known as Tomb 813 in Brünnow's classification, it was given its present name by a loculus cover slab, found in the vicinity in the 19th century; the inscription sculpted on the stone bears the epitaph of Uneishu, minister of the queen Shaquilat. She was the wife of Aretas IV and mother of Rabbel II, during whose childhood she reigned for six years. This and other fragments of inscriptions found inside have allowed the monument to be dated to a period between 70 and 76 AD. The large number of loculi present in the funerary chamber would suggest that the tomb was used for at least three decades by Uneishu's direct relatives, in keeping with a widely ascertained custom. This rather elaborate tomb is preceded by a courtyard and has a triclinium, visible to the left.

THE THEATER

Not far from the Tomb of Uneishu, on the left of the Outer Siq, the visitor's attention is drawn to the huge auditorium of the theater, one of the most spectacular rock structures in the Rose-red City. Despite the monument's standard Roman plan (with a perfectly semi-circular orchestra), its date of origin is not certain. It is thought to have been built during the reign of Aretas IV (8 BC-40 AD), when Petra was still independent, but already strongly influenced by the art and

tangible evidence of this gigantic excavation work; the orientation of the surviving façades, visible to the right and left, indicate where the above-mentioned street ran.

It is conceivable that these vast apertures were in fact walled up and that the filling collapsed during the earthquakes that struck the city repeatedly, although there is no visible evidence to support this hypothesis.

As it appears today, the auditorium, most of which is carved into the rock, has 45 rows of seats, divided into three horizontal sections and six vertical ones by steps that allowed the spectators to reach their seats.

An ingenious drainage system – achieved with complex channelling – carried the rainwater away. The theater is thought to have seated between 6,000 and 8,500 people, but some writers raise this limit to 10,000, a third of the city's entire population. The orchestra, 82 feet in

culture of Rome. In this initial phase the theater must have reached the height of the second annular passage visible today. This large building reflects Petra's wealth. Later, after Trajan had annexed the Nabatean kingdom to the empire in 106, the structure was extended greatly at the expense of those tombs along the road behind it. They were ruthlessly carved away to accommodate a new auditorium sector.

The huge holes left halfway up the back wall – what remains of the original burial chambers – are

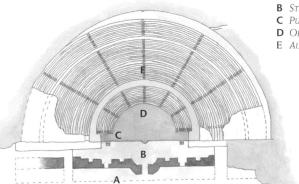

A FRONS SCENAE
B STAGE
C PULPITUM
D ORCHESTRA
E AUDITORIUM

diameter, was also carved from the
emerging rock. The stage platform
was raised according to Roman
custom but only a few traces have
survived earthquakes and floods.

The well-restored stage,
fronted by the traditional *pulpitum* (a
low wall with niches), was 124 feet
wide. Behind it the *frons scenae* (the
back stage), with three entrances,
must have had two colonnaded
levels and been sumptuously
enriched with frescoes, statues
and marble friezes.

Two barrel-vaulted passages,

once plastered and painted, are visible
at the sides of the stage and led via
covered passages and steps to the
orchestra and the auditorium. From
the exterior, the theater must have
looked very somber and solid, a blind
wall no less than 82 feet high and
approximately 195-210 feet long, that
completely blocked the view of the
auditorium.

The great earthquake of 363
probably destroyed the theatre,
but many scholars believe that
performances had already ceased to
be staged here some time earlier.

Petra

58 top Detail of the
Tomb of Sextius
Florentinus; it has an
arched pediment adorned
with a gorgon's head.

58 centre An unusual
view of the Jebel el
Kubtha rock face, in
which are carved the
façades of the Royal
Tombs.

58 bottom Detail of the
entrance to the Urn
Tomb, showing the
Doric frieze re-
elaborated in respect of
local style.

59 The Urn Tomb,
fronted by a short
colonnade and high
two-storey
substructures.

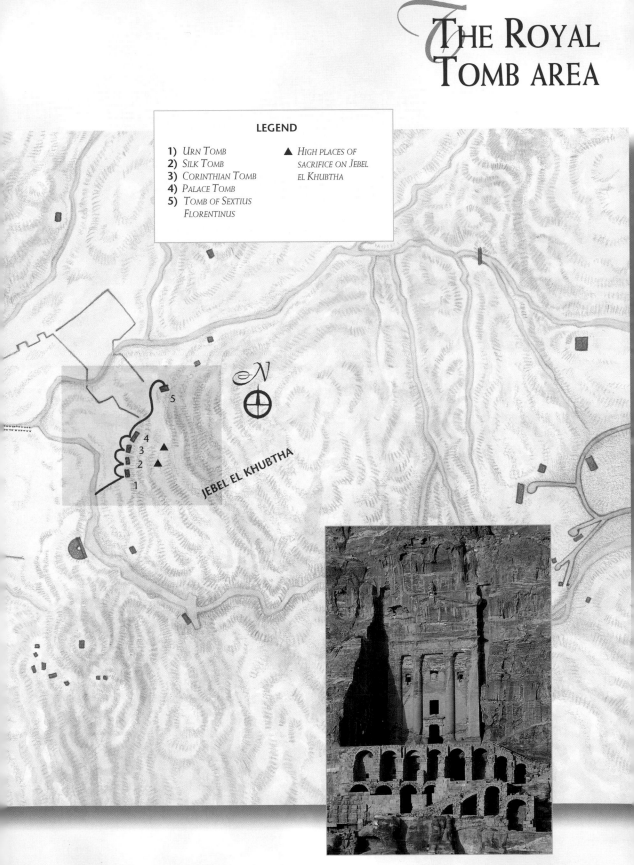

THE ROYAL TOMB AREA

LEGEND

1) *Urn Tomb*
2) *Silk Tomb*
3) *Corinthian Tomb*
4) *Palace Tomb*
5) *Tomb of Sextius Florentinus*

▲ *High places of sacrifice on Jebel el Khubtha*

N

JEBEL EL KHUBTHA

59

THE URN TOMB

60 top A large courtyard, enclosed on the east side by cloisters with plain Doric columns, fronts the Urn Tomb. The loculi seen in the photograph are of a later date than the tomb. The columns on the west side are missing.

Not far from the theater and just past the refreshment kiosk, on the right-hand side of the road that leads from the Siq to the center of Petra, an easily spotted path climbs up the rock face of Jebel el Khubtha to the so-called "Royal Tombs." Although there is no written evidence or archaeological find to confirm that these are indeed the burial places of the Nabatean sovereigns, their size – and

platform, the arches visible today being all that remains. The soaring façade is structured like the front of a temple and framed by two corner pillars against which are set quarter-columns; the two central half-columns on the podium flank the entrance, surmounted by a Doric frieze (the metopes of which are replaced with circles) and a small pediment. The upper part of the intercolumns contains three loculi but

60 bottom The façades of the Royal Tombs, on the side of Jebel el-Khubtha, appear as you emerge from the Outer Siq. Together with the Khasneh and the Deir, the Urn Tomb (top, left) is certainly the most famous monument in Petra and its high position, colonnaded courtyard and slender façade make it instantly recognizable.

consequently, the high estimated cost of their construction – would suggest that this assumption is correct.

The most striking if by no means the largest of these structures is the Urn Tomb, easily recognized by the great substructures that front it and the extraordinary way the façade is set back from the natural profile of the mountain. Similar in plan to the Petra Forum Rest House tomb, it is preceded by a large courtyard, 70 feet wide and enclosed on two sides by low colonnades dug into the rocks. The front of this open space was widened with the construction of a raised

only the middle one has preserved its closing stone, adorned with a much-deteriorated male head and torso, identified by some as the effigy of King Malchus II (40-70 AD).

The large tripartitioned attic story (the lower architrave immediately above the capitals also reveals the presence of four bas-relief busts, presumably deities) sustains a pediment with tympanum devoid of decoration. On the very top of this pediment is the acroterion, in the form of an urn, after which the tomb was named.

Although, as always, very austere and devoid of ornamentation, the

60-61 The substructures at the front of the building were built to support a platform that increased the surface area of the courtyard and gave the tomb a monumental flight of steps. Some archaeologists believe they are coeval to the tomb, others date them to the Byzantine period. Nevertheless, their purpose is still unknown.

61 top The Urn Tomb is a splendid example of a pedimented building, its façade imitating a distyle in antis temple. On the basis of stylistic and architectural analysis this is thought to be the tomb of King Malchus II (40-70 AD) and his family. Recently however, it has been suggested that it may be the tomb of Aretas IV (8 BC-40 AD). Unfortunately, the three loculi are empty and there are no specific elements to support one or the other of the theories.

61 bottom In 447 the Urn Tomb was turned into a church, as shown by an inscription in Greek painted on the wall beside the niche in the left wall of the underground chamber. This records the consecration of the building by the bishop Jason. The holes seen in the floor in front of the central apse housed the small pillars that supported the balustrade all around the altar, typical of the tradition of the Byzantine period. The pulpit stood to the right of the altar.

interior deserves a visit; it is a massive chamber, approximately 62 feet wide and 56 deep and the unplastered walls look as though they have been covered with watered silk. It was probably used as a *triclinium* and altered when the monument was converted to a church, in 447. At this time the triclinial beds were destroyed, the floor levelled, a large window opened above the door, two side doors hewn out and the back wall – which originally had four niches – was given a sort of *arcosolium* apse by joining the two central recesses.

A SUBSTRUCTURES
B COURTYARD
C PORTICOES WITH DORIC COLUMNS
D LARGE CHAMBER OR TRICLINIUM
E ARCOSOLIA
F NICHES

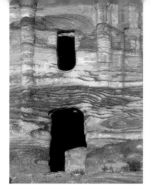

62 left The striking appearance of the Silk Tomb, also known as the Rainbow Tomb for the multitude of colors in its fine sandstone façade, has stirred the imagination of many writers and poets.

62 center The beautiful color combinations seen in the bank of fine sandstone lying beside the Silk Tomb are highlighted by the low rays of sunset or after a storm, when the rock is still wet.

62 left This picture permits a comparison between the façade of the Silk Tomb and an adjacent crow-stepped tomb; not only is the former seen to be brightly colored, it also has a more complex architectural design, particularly evident on the attic level.

62-63 Unfortunately, the position of the Corinthian Tomb has done little to help its preservation. Despite being seriously damaged, it remains extremely interesting for its remarkable blend of different architectural styles.

THE SILK TOMB

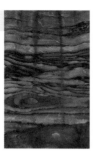

A few yards past the Urn Tomb (keeping the rock face to your right), you come to a monument that is considered one of the most photogenic subjects in Petra. This is the Silk Tomb, thus named for the spectacular polychrome veining of the stone it was dug into. The finely streaked sandstone contains bands of color that range from powder pink, salmon and white, to pale blue, ochre and saffron yellow, creating an enchantingly beautiful spectrum. As well as for its brilliant coloring, the tomb deserves careful observation for the elaborate crow-step façade which is still visible although fairly eroded. The lower part is marked by four prominent pilaster strips, topped with the characteristic Nabatean capitals; the lateral intercolumns frame two niches which, quite unusually, contain numerous relief figures, now too worn to be identified with certainty. The attic level, that sustains the Assyrian-style battlements, is divided by four short pilaster strips with capitals in line with those below; this lend a highly animated appearance to the whole.

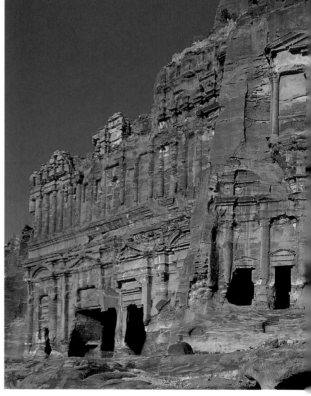

THE CORINTHIAN TOMB

Standing adjacent to the Silk Tomb, the Corinthian Tomb is a monument of considerable architectural interest but unfortunately has suffered more than others from the ravages of time and the elements. Exposed to strong winds and falling rocks, the structure is greatly damaged but nonetheless remains impressive: 80 feet wide by approximately 92 high. It was given its name by two of the first visitors to Petra – the Englishmen Irby and Mangles – because of the style of the capitals, similar to those of the Khasneh. For its similarity to this building, the Corinthian Tomb is often hastily dismissed as a sort of bad copy. Actually, devoid of projections and avant-corps and hence purely decorative, more careful inspection of the architecture of the Corinthian Tomb reveals that it differs greatly from the Khasneh, and the similarity lies mainly in the division of the upper story. As a whole it is far more precise to say that it represents an attempted compromise between traditional Nabatean and imported Hellenistic styles. The entire lower order was clearly designed in accordance with traditional local canons: the very squat half-columns, the semi-circular crowning of the main portal, the broken pediment and the repetition in the large attic story of horizontal (cornices) and vertical

(pilaster strips) lines closely resemble the Bab al Siq Triclinium. The upper story, with its two semi-pediments and central tholos, floral capitals and the soaring verticality of the whole is instead a tribute to Hellenistic taste and the Alexandrian imprint already applied to the Khasneh. This eclectic combination may appear hardly organic and even discordant to our eyes, but the ancient inhabitants of Petra may not have shared this opinion. Standing in a privileged position in line with the great Colonnade Street, at the height of its splendor this building must have been a backdrop of considerable scenographic effect.

Once again, the interior is disappointing and, as it is also difficult to reach, you are advised against visiting it. Strangely, the doors lead to many different-sized chambers, separate from one another. Given the presence in the main room of numerous niches for deposition, it is thought to have been a collective tomb, destined to accommodate the remains of a high-ranking figure and his family. In the absence of inscriptions or other historical evidence and on the basis of mere supposition related to its architectural style, some believe that this person was king Aretas III whereas other historians think it was Malchus II, making the dating of the monument open to debate.

A *FUNERARY CHAMBERS*
B *LOCULI*

63 top right and center As illustrated clearly in these photographs, the two smaller doors in the left-hand intercolumns, not balanced by similar ones on the right, constitute an incongruous disturbance to the symmetry of the Corinthian Tomb's façade.
Another extremely anomalous presence is that of the two large windows (only the right one is still intact) set at the sides of the main doorway. They seem unrelated to the presumed funerary use of the monument and it is thought that they may have been opened in the Byzantine period, when the building was adapted for a different use.

63 bottom right The upper order of the tomb, with the tholos between two semi-pediments, betrays obvious links with the late Hellenistic architectural tradition already experimented with in the Khasneh. Unlike the latter, however, the Corinthian Tomb is totally devoid of group statues or bas-relief figures.

64-65 *This is how the façade of the Corinthian Tomb must have appeared before being disfigured by earthquakes and centuries of wind erosion.*

The two small doors to the left open onto as many small chambers and the main doorway leads to a room 40 feet by 30 feet. If this really was a burial chamber, the two windows and the "slits" in the intercolumns to the right, are inconsistent and may have been opened at a later date, for an as-yet unclear reuse of the tomb.

65 right The photograph highlights the serious damage caused to the Corinthian Tomb by the ravages of time.

The section of façade surrounding the main doorway seems particularly eroded, such that the opening looks like a natural cave. Inside the door, there is a great gaping hole in the floor of the main room, making access almost impossible. There would seem to be an underground chamber below and this may have been uncovered when part of the walls collapsed as a result of centuries of unfavorable weather conditions. Nonetheless, the cavity, blocked by rubble and never properly investigated, may merely have been produced by erosion. Again, because the monument has been so eroded, it is very hard to say whether the room to the left of the large doorway was a separate one, or part of the main chamber — a sort of very large niche. The plan drawn by Laborde, who saw the tomb in 1828, showed just three unconnected rooms.

66-67 As it has been
pointed out by several
writers – including
Browning – the façade
of the Palace Tomb
resembles the frons scenae
of a theater, more so
than any other in Petra.

66 bottom The picture
shows how the attic
storey (or "third story")
presents the unusual
juxtaposition of
decorative elements
repeated again and
again.

The last of the Royal Tombs true
and proper is the colossal Palace
Tomb, situated right beside the
Corinthian Tomb. Although the
façade has lost most of its upper part,
it is still the most imposing in Petra,
160 feet wide and approximately 150
feet high.

This name is used because by
tradition the architecture of this tomb
is thought to imitate that of the large
Hellenistic palaces. Although some
believe it was inspired by the Golden
House in Rome, Nero's sumptuous
palace, there is no specific evidence to
bear out this supposition. It is clearly
very different from the other known
pediment tombs of the Nabatean
City; indeed it can be considered
unique, for the stereometric plan, its
decoration and the striking difference
between the ground floor and the
upper levels. Fronted by a large
balcony of sorts, and originally
entered up steps cut into the
sandstone, the four huge doors are
framed by half-pillars with Nabatean
capitals below double molding with a
smooth frieze. Each aperture stands
between two pillars flanked by a
quarter column and "horn" capitals,
which support a double-dentilled
cornice that soars vertically; the side
ones support a pediment with
triangular tympanum and the inner
ones a semi-circular pediment. The
whole appears majestic and well
balanced. The second story, separated
by a highly unusual and completely
smooth unbroken entablature, seems
to be the result of a change in the
original project.

The architectural decoration consists of the juxtaposition of repeated identical elements, intended to create a disconcerting overall effect. The 18 half-columns, also with Nabatean capitals, are not at all aligned with the vertical elements of the story below. Divided in pairs, they support a double, alternating recessed and advanced entablature without frieze. Above this was a third story – or attic – divided into several registers by short pilaster strips which were the continuation of the half-columns of the lower story. Except for the right-hand section, this story was constructed in masonry, as the front of

67 top right The pediments of the large entrances, two with tympanum and two arched, are also reminiscent of Hellenistic architecture and the Imperial-Roman archi-tecture widely seen in Asia Minor in partic-ular. The dating of the building is based merely on the examination of the structural and decorative characteristics and is still open to debate.

A TERRACE
B FUNERARY CHAMBERS

67 bottom The 18 semi-columns that mark the second story evidently imitate a portico; this uncommon feature may have been taken from Roman-Hellenistic architectural tradition (as seen, for instance, in the Agora Gate or the Nymphaeum of Miletus, as well as in the Library of Celsus, at Ephesus and in the Gymnasium of Side). The play of chiaroscuro created by the alternation of advanced and recessed masses, today scarcely visible, may once have been emphasized with a layer of plaster.

the cliff was too low for the whole building. Unfortunately, much of this, built with large stones, collapsed during earthquakes. High up to the right, there appears to be a fourth story, slightly set back from the vertical line of the façade and marked by pilaster strips partially hewn into the rock. In the spring of 1998, this writer noticed what looks like the bases of as many columns in line with each of the above pilaster strips, speculating that the façade may have ended with a continuous gallery sustaining a crowning entablature. This is merely a hypothesis and awaits investigation by the experts.

Yet again, the interior of the Palace Tomb is quite bare, the four doors leading to as many unadorned rooms, which were undoubtedly originally plastered and frescoed. Only the middle two chambers are open to one another. There is no documentary evidence, but this is thought possibly to have been the tomb of Rabbel II, the last Nabatean king.

68-69 The drawing shows how the massive Palace Tomb may originally have looked. Up to the upper cornice of the attic story (or third story), its reconstruction presents no great difficulties because the upper-right-hand corner of the monument is relatively well preserved. This gives a good idea of what the structure must have looked like before the constructed masonry collapsed. The top story is more difficult to picture. The way the rock was cut (to the right) at the top and the presence of the pilaster strips carved in the recessed story would suggest that the building originally rose a good bit higher.

Halfway up the second story, a large natural fissure, on the left side of the monument, was filled, with a wall resting on a relieving arch, still visible. Such a large substructure must have had to sustain considerable weight while what remains of the façade betrays a programmed repetition of identical structural elements. The way the top story, partially dug in the stone, is set back would seem to avail the hypothesis of a gallery, a replica (three-dimensional this time) of the mock colonnade on the second story. This gallery would date the Palace Tomb to the time of Trajan, or at least to a period after the Roman conquest.

68 top The façade clearly denotes the presence of six niches in the intercolumns on the second story. Their function is unknown but some writers believe they contained marble slabs bearing memorial inscriptions; these, however, would have been practically impossible to read and their presence would have broken the rhythm of solids and voids suggested by the mock colonnade. The mystery therefore remains.

68 bottom The use of Nabatean capitals bears witness to the syncretism between local traditions and imported architectural tastes.

THE TOMB OF SEXTIUS FLORENTINUS

A few minutes from the Palace Tomb is a monument of considerable interest, although very small compared with the giants described previously. Technically speaking, this is not one of the Royal Tombs, but its importance and beauty prompt its inclusion on this itinerary. Follow the track that descends into Wadi Mataha, on the side of Jebel el Khubtha, which drops to become a sort of promontory. To the left you will see the ruins (here hardly visible) of the Roman-Byzantine ring of walls, while to the right a spectacular

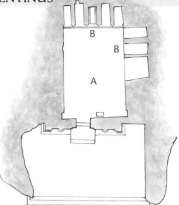

A *FUNERARY CHAMBER*
B *LOCULI*

70 right The tomb of Sextius Florentinus shows the continuing application of Hellenistic architectural language in Petra even after the Roman conquest.

71 The gorgon's head that adorns the semi-circular tympanum seems to be based on a similar decoration on the pediment of the Khasneh. This would confirm that the latter does not date from the time of Hadrian's visit (129-130), as the tomb of Sextius Florentinus dates just from 129 or 130.

70 top left Half-pillars with quarter columns leaning against them are very common in Petra. The composite style of the Tomb of Sextius Florentinus denotes local, Hellenistic and very marginal Roman influence.

70 bottom left Although he was Roman, the Governor Sextius Florentinus must have loved the city in which he spent the last years of his life; this is confirmed by the appearance of his tomb, totally consistent with the repertoire of Nabatean architecture.

flight of steps cut into the stone rises towards the "High Place of Sacrifice" on Jebel el Khubtha.

A few yards farther on, at the end of the northernmost tip of the rocky massif, appears the splendid façade of the Tomb of Sextius Florentinus. Hardly ever in the sunlight and much ruined by the passage of time, it conveys a mournful elegance and, in its most eroded parts, displays a stunning range of colors. It is highly elaborate and divided into two orders: the lower one has a doorway framed by four pilaster strips and topped with a pediment and triangular tympanum; the upper one, above the continuous entablature, on which is a large arch, has an attic story divided into several registers by four cornices and short pilaster strips and crowned with a triangular pediment. The bas-relief that adorns the semi-circular

tympanum, surmounted by an eagle, depicts a gorgon's head set against a background of foliage. A porticoed courtyard probably extended in front of the building, as indicated by some fragments of column half-buried in the sand. The interior consists of a funerary chamber, the back wall of which is divided by pilaster strips framing five loculi; another three loculi open in the right-hand wall.

This is the only tomb in Petra that can be dated with relative accuracy, thanks to a very worn funerary inscription in Latin carved on the lower entablature. The text states that his son dedicated the burial place to Sextius Florentinus, legate of Hadrian and Proprietor of the Province of Arabia between 126 and 129 or 130 AD.

Petra

AL HABIS

WADI

MOUSA

JEBEL EI

N

6

7

5

4

2

1

3

KHUBTHA

72 top Detail of the Columbarium, one of Petra's most remarkable and mysterious monuments.

72 bottom A fragment of a Corinthian capital, of clear Graeco-Roman influence.

72 centre Colonnade Street – or the Cardo Maximus – with some of the columns erected after the Roman conquest.

73 Another view of Colonnade Street, showing pieces of the bas-reliefs that used to decorate the Temenos Gate (left).

LEGEND

1) COLONNADE STREET
2) TEMENOS GATE
3) PHARAOH'S COLUMN
4) KASR EL BINT

5) OLD MUSEUM
6) NEW MUSEUM
7) TEMPLE OF THE WINGED LIONS

THE COLONNADE STREET

At the present stage of archaeological excavation, what remains of the city proper extends along the course of Wadi Mousa, between Jebel el Khubtha and the al Habis rock. The ruins start just past the lower mouth of the Outer Siq, to the left, approximately 400 yards from the Theater.

The urban layout consisted mainly of an expanse of small flat-roofed houses and occupied much of the valley,

A	COLONNADE STREET	**L**	BATHS
B	NYMPHAEUM	**M**	TEMENOS GATE
C	SHRINE	**N**	SMALL TEMPLE
D	UPPER MARKET	**O**	TEMENOS
E	MIDDLE MARKET	**P**	KASR EL BINT
F	LOWER MARKET	**Q**	GREAT ALTAR
G	PROPYLAEUM	**R**	TEMPLE OF THE
H	GREAT TEMPLE		WINGED LIONS
I	ROMAN HOUSE	**S**	ROYAL PALACE
J	PHARAOH'S RUINS	**T**	BYZANTINE TOWER
K	PHARAOH'S COLUMN	**U**	BYZANTINE CHURCH

now reduced to a stretch of sand, bushes and well-squared stone ashlars. Two strong rings of walls with incorporated towers, very probably built towards the end of the first century BC, defended the city to the north and south. Several archaeologists believe that a considerable number of ancient structures still lie quite well preserved under a foot or so of rubble and sand. If this is so, future generations will be kept busy. At the moment, however, it is Colonnade Street that attracts visitors' attention.

The street commences at the point where Wadi Mataha joins the seasonal river coming from the Outer Siq, but it probably used to start slightly farther east. From this point on, the waterway is, by common accord, once more known as Wadi Mousa and passes through the entire urban area from east to west. Colonnade Street runs parallel to it for approximately 300 yards, and sections of the strong embankments built by the Nabateans to contain the *wadi* can still be seen. This had probably become the city's main

thoroughfare well before the reign of Aretas IV, but this monarch gave it its first monumental design. It seems certain, however, that the stone paving and the two colonnaded porticoes of which some sections have survived can be attributed to the emperor Trajan (98-117 AD), who had conquered the Nabatean capital and wanted to embellish it according to western tastes. Having, in keeping with Roman tradition, adopted the name of *Cardo Maximus*, the street became the bustling center of the metropolis. All the major

74 top *Colonnade Street was paved and flanked on both sides by colonnaded porticoes, beneath which were shops and bars. The picture shows, to the left, one of the flights of steps that led to the markets.*

74-75 *This sweeping view covers the entire length of Colonnade Street with the Temenos Gate near the foreground and the Great Temple compound to the right; the Temple of the Winged Lions is seen to the left.*

75 top *The fact that the paving of Colonnade Street – or Cardo Maximus – dates from Roman times was confirmed in 1958 when a dedicatory inscription to Trajan dated 114 AD was found.*

public buildings stood along it and business was conducted, money exchanged and people ate and drank here chatting idly in the refreshing shade of its porticoes. Colonnade Street starts at the point where a lone tree grows on the ruins of a *nymphaeum*, a large public fountain, supplied by the aqueduct from Moses' Spring. On the left-hand side, preceded by a wide flight of steps, were three large markets, but these are now reduced to heaps of rubble and are very difficult to decipher.

75 bottom *This picture clearly shows that, seen from Colonnade Street, the façades of the Royal Tombs acted as a sort of spectacular backdrop. The columns seen to the left, along the street were returned to their original position by the Department of Antiquities in 1960.*

75

76 top A wide flight of steps in the western sector of Colonnade Street leads through the remains of the Propylaeum to the vast sacred precinct in which the Great Temple stood.

76-77 This is an aerial view of the monuments that stand along Colonnade Street, which ends to the left with the Temenos Gate. At the bottom left are the Great Temple and, to the right, the Roman House. Visible at the top left are the Temple of the Winged Lions and, to the right, the Byzantine Church.

the Greek goddess assimilated by the Nabateans into Al Uzza) mentioned in a document from 124 AD is sheer conjecture. Behind the Great Temple, at the top of the hill, are the ruins of what must have been a palace, temple or a monumental structure of some importance. The ruins are known as the "Pharaoh's Ruins" and, as usual, this name is based on a Bedouin legend. Here the eye is drawn to a solitary column of rather surreal appearance not far away, standing beside another long fallen to the ground. The "Pharaoh's Column" and its companion must have formed some part of the nearby complex, although their purpose is not at all clear. In 1988, excavation work started to the east of the Pharaoh's Ruins on a large house from the Roman period, built on the foundations of an older dwelling; the Roman building, on two storys, was probably knocked to the ground by the earthquake of 363 AD.

At the end of Colonnade Street, on the left, an impressive flight of steps climbs to a vast quadrangular terrace, once passing through a monumental propylaeum, the foundations of which can still be seen. This courtyard, surrounded on its east and west sides by colonnaded porticoes ending with two exedra, was the *temenos* of a great peripteral tetrastyle temple, which was entered up a flight of steps that filled the entire south side of the courtyard. The sacred building stood at the center of a second colonnaded courtyard, in a spectacular raised position. Although the monument – conventionally known as the "Great Temple" – is still being excavated, it almost certainly dates from the middle of the first century AD. The Nabatean-style capitals with floral motifs and architectural fragments found *in situ* relate to a building phase prior to Roman domain. As can easily be deduced from the position on the ground of the sections of columns, the Temple collapsed after an earthquake. Some finds seem to demonstrate that the sanctuary remained in use until the sixth century and the earthquake was therefore probably that which struck Petra around the middle of the same century. That the temple was consecrated to the goddess Al Uzza and was the *Aphrodiseion* (a temple dedicated to Aphrodite,

76 bottom left *The position of the sections of columns lying on the ground reveals that the Great Temple and annexed structures collapsed after an earthquake.*

76 bottom right *The Roman House was built in a position overlooking the city.*

77 top *Because of its unusual form, the "Pharaoh's Column" is also known as Zibb Faraoun but "zibb" is a vulgar name for phallus, and if you say it you may provoke the mirth, or worse, of the Bedouins. This name should be avoided in their presence.*

77 bottom *The overall concept of the Great temple - the temenos preceded by the propilei, the great periptero surrounded by a colonnaded portico, the spectacular effect of the complex - is Hellenistic in origin and is present in many cities in the Near East.*

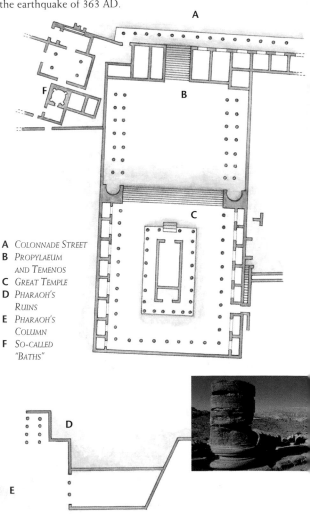

A COLONNADE STREET
B PROPYLAEUM
   AND TEMENOS
C GREAT TEMPLE
D PHARAOH'S
   RUINS
E PHARAOH'S
   COLUMN
F SO-CALLED
   "BATHS"

78 left On the motab was perhaps venerated the simulacrum of the goddess Al Uzza, to whom it is presumed that the temple of the Winged Lions was consecrated.

78-79 The Temple of the Winged Lions was probably erected in the first half of the first century BC and then repeatedly altered. The picture shows how the

excavations have uncovered, in the area around the building, the foundations of various rooms, including some craft workshops.

78 top The inside of the Temple of the Winged Lions is marked by a real forest of columns; according to Nabatean building customs, these are very close to each other and are made of very small drums.

THE TEMPLE OF THE WINGED LIONS

On the westernmost part of Colonnade Street, on a rise opposite the Great Temple, stands the ruins of the "Temple of the Winged Lions." The monument, of which the massive foundations are still visible, was originally approached on a bridge built across Wadi Mousa. It was preceded by two vast terraces on different levels, the lower of which was apparently surrounded by a colonnaded portico. Typically Nabatean in design, the temple itself consisted of a large portico *in antis* erected on strong vaulted substructures (uncovered during the

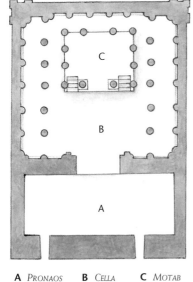

A PRONAOS   B CELLA   C MOTAB

excavations commenced in 1974), which led to the cella through a wide portal. The walls of the square-plan interior were marked by half-columns framing deep niches. Five free-standing columns, in line with the pilaster strips, were aligned some way from the side walls, to form two aisles. At the center was a high square platform, surrounded by 12 columns in the manner of a peristyle, reached via two flights of steps on the front, between the external intercolumns. The platform, which served as an altar, was called a *motab*. The interior, entered from the rear, contained a small chamber, perhaps used as storage for sacred ornaments and vestments. The floor of the temple was covered with marble slabs, as was the *motab* and the base of the walls; the upper half, the shafts of the

columns and perhaps also the ceiling were covered with painted stuccowork. The monument was named after the unusual decoration on some capitals found during excavations; the usual Corinthian volutes were replaced with the figures of winged lions. Pieces of masonry are visible to the east of the temple, scattered over an area full of architectural fragments and regular-shaped stone ashlars. A large monumental structure stood here, fronted by a terrace approached from Colonnade Street across a bridge and similar to that of the Temple of the Winged Lions. Although the area has never been systematically explored, the building has been given the charming name of Royal Palace. This definition is, however, not very convincing.

THE TEMENOS GATE

Colonnade Street ends to the west, towards the al Habis rock, with the remains of a three-vaulted monumental arch. Razed by an earthquake, this monument has been partially and painstakingly reconstructed and may be further restored using original material found nearby. Until a short time ago the ruins were thought to belong to a triumphal arch erected at the end of the *Cardo Maximus* in honor of the emperor Trajan (98-117 AD), but recent studies have contradicted this theory. It has now been established that, despite resembling a triumphal arch in form, this structure was actually a gate, with heavy wooden doors, as demonstrated by a stone curb placed across the central opening and the sockets in which the metal hinges rotated.

This gate separated Colonnade Street, and hence the bustle of

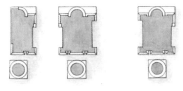

everyday life, from the silent *temenos*, overlooked by Kasr el Bint, one of Petra's most important temples. *Temenos* is a Greek term used in antiquity to define a consecrated, enclosed open-air space where ceremonies in honor of the deities were held. The fact that the three-vault gate served this vast square is confirmed by its position, slightly oblique to the line of Colonnade Street, but perfectly aligned with the short sides of the *temenos*. Archaeological excavations have shown that this gate, built in Roman times (which explains its unusual shape) after the completion of Colonnade Street, stands on an older structure that served the same purpose. The monument's spectacular effect was heightened by its richly carved decorations and the four free-standing columns on the front, facing the *Cardo Maximus*.

The great Temenos gate, flanked on its short sides by two buildings still being studied, provided access to a vast rectangular square set on an east-west axis. The left-hand "tower" acted as a vestibule for a colonnaded chamber which opened onto three rooms, in part subterranean and with domed ceilings; these are not yet entirely open to visitors because they are still being excavated. At the time of their discovery they were thought to be part of a bath complex, but it now seems clear that this was not the case. They were probably part of a larger religious building, perhaps connected with the Great Temple. On the subject of unresolved dilemmas, fragments of carvings and some panels carved with the effigies of gods of the Greco-Roman pantheon (two of these are reproduced on pages 12 and 13) have also been found at various stages around the Temenos gate. Accurate

80-81 Of all the buildings constructed that were the urban fabric of Petra, the Kasr el Bint is the best preserved, alone in having resisted the earthquakes that razed the rest of the Nabatean capital.

80 bottom In recent years, the Kasr el Bint has been subjected to proper restoration work, which has addressed mainly the rear southeast corner and the steps built into the back wall.

A PRONAOS
B CELLA
C ADYTON
D SIDE CELLAS
E STEPS

versions of western models made by local artists, it is not yet clear whether these were part of the decoration of the gate or of an adjacent building. On the south side (on the left arriving from Colonnade Street) the *temenos* was closed by a long retaining wall; two unbroken rows of seats stood against this, where worshippers used to sit during the sacred celebrations. The north side must have presented a similar arrangement but, once the embankment erected by the Nabateans had worn away, the disastrous floods of

Nabatean inscription to king Aretas IV (8 BC-40 AD); as this must have been the base of a statue, it is thought to be one of a row of statues on this side. The discovery of this inscription has made it possible to date the present design of the *temenos* to the first years of the first century AD.

Standing at the back of the great square, to the left of the north-south axis, is the most conspicuous constructed monument still visible in Petra – the Kasr el Bint, a great tetrastyle temple *in antis*. Its full name, Kasr el Bint Faraoun or "Palace of the Pharaoh's daughter," is yet again the fruit of a Bedouin legend totally devoid of historical foundation.

Attributed until a few years ago to the Roman period, the monument actually dates from the second half of the first century BC, probably from the reign of Obodas III (30-8 BC). Because of its superior position and majestic structure, it is common opinion that the temple was consecrated to the two most important local deities, Dusares and Al Uzza, although there is no evidence to support this theory.

The wall ran all the way around the *temenos* in the manner of a peribolos and then continued to the east, where it

Wadi Mousa eliminated all traces of such structures. Also on the south side of the square are the remains of an altar, a small prostyle temple (raised above the level of the *temenos*), a small water basin and a monumental gate, leading to a flight of steps, the function of which is unknown. Set in the back wall is a block of sandstone bearing a

formed an exedra before meeting up with the north side of the square.

The remains of a huge sacrificial altar, preceded by steps and now just under 10 feet high, stand between the façade of Kasr el Bint and the bed of Wadi Mousa. Given its position, this was obviously closely connected with the temple.

81 left On the left door on the façade, part of the stucco decoration is still visible; the niche to the right of the door perhaps housed a slab with an inscription or a holy image.

81 top right The great doorway of the temple is still surmounted by an arch, which neither the earthquake of 363, nor the subsequent tremors managed to destroy. This is a relieving arch which served the purpose of easing the pressure exercised by the masonry on the lintel of the door below. As this was a monolith, it could not resist the tremors and shattered.

81 bottom right In the adyton, that is the holiest part of the temple, the image of the deity was housed.

82-83 This is how the temple known today as Kasr el Bint must have looked. With a square plan, built in ashlars of sandstone bound with mortar, it measured 105 feet per side and rose on a high podium fronted visible on the rear wall of the temple. From the great pronaos, three steps led to the cella: This vast rectangular hall was illuminated by two large windows, opened high on the short sides. Three adjacent by a flight of steps covered with slabs of marble. The overall height was approximately 95 feet. The façade was of the in antis type with four ungrooved columns crowned with capitals, perhaps similar to those of the Khasneh; in the frieze on the entablature, the metopes consisting of busts of deities alternated with pairs of rosettes. Unfortunately, as it can be seen in the detail at the bottom left, the medallions containing the bas-reliefs were obliterated by the iconoclasts; only the metope depicting Helios (today in the Archaeo-logical Museum in Amman) has survived intact. The external face was covered with a thick layer of modelled and painted stucco: part of this decoration (picture top right) is still rooms opened onto the cella: the central one was the adyton, which housed the effigy of the deity. Approximately a foot and a half higher than the cella, it was reached via two side staircases; the front was bordered by two pillars surmounted by an arch, whereas the walls were adorned with half-columns. The side rooms – in which were held the symposia in honor of the gods – were articulated on two stories. In each of these, two columns between pillars supported the mezzanine floor, reached by a staircase built into the back wall. One or both staircases led to the flat roof where the holy ceremonies were officiated. At a later stage, on the east and west sides of the temple were constructed two colonnaded porticoes.

THE UNFINISHED TOMB

The impressive rock of al Habis, defined as the "citadel" of Petra by some and the "acropolis" by others, rises behind Kasr el Bint. Much of the city of Petra lay at its base and extended up the rocky slopes. Many of the caves dug in its sides were actually rock dwellings and some minor traces of their plaster and wall decorations have been preserved. One of the most interesting monuments in this sector is, however, the so-called "Unfinished Tomb," already mentioned in the chapter on architectural models, which provides a fundamental explanation of the techniques adopted by the Nabatean workers. This monument shows that, after the rock face had been duly squared, the excavation work proceeded from the top downwards. The only completed parts of this hypogeum are the architrave and the four capitals below it: two to crown the lateral half-pillars and two for the central columns. Once they arrived at this stage, the stone cutters started to hollow out the internal chamber, leaving a diaphragm which would later be used for the shafts of the columns. Had it been finished, the façade would have had the appearance of a huge portico *in antis*, the largest of its type in the Rose-red City. Why work was interrupted remains a mystery. The door cut at ground level is manifestly the fruit of later intervention, as the opening is set perpendicular to the spot where a column should have been.

84 center This detail shows how, after having outlined architrave and capitals of the great façade in antis, the Nabatean stone cutters had already started to dig the internal chamber of the Unfinished Tomb.

THE COLUMBARIUM

84 bottom Without doubt, the Columbarium has a strange appearance. The largest recesses carved in the façade may have contained divine effigies and in the niches all around, the worshippers would therefore have placed their ex votos, but this is merely a supposition.

Not far past the façade of the Unfinished Tomb, towards the southernmost tip of al Habis, is what is perhaps the most mysterious monument in the whole Nabatean capital. The hypogeum known as the Columbarium has, in fact, been interpreted in various manners but no plausible explanation has so far been found. Quite simply, no one knows the purpose of this extravagant rock structure. The walls of the façade, set back from the rock profile, and the internal chamber are literally covered with square niches, arranged tidily in rows one above the other. The effect is truly disconcerting. *Columbarium* is a Latin word used to indicate a particular type of burial chamber with semi-circular or square niches on the walls containing cinerary urns, and thus resembling a dove-cote or pigeon house. The definition would seem to apply, but the niches here are too shallow to house any type

84-85 As can be seen in this picture, the niches are not cubical in shape, and the back surface slants forwar. This would have made them totally unsuited to hold urns, however small.

85 top Many have wondered whether the Columbarium was not just that, a dove-cote. But the niches are too small even for this purpose and, moreover, there are no traces of guano.

of urn. Some believe these small recesses have a religious function and that the worshippers placed votive tablets, tiny baetyli or, perhaps, simulacra of deities in some form inside them. This is similar to modern sanctuaries, where the believers amass huge quantities of *ex votos*. It is a lovely idea but there is no proof to support it. The mystery, therefore, remains.

85 bottom
The Columbarium remains an inexplicable mystery; it is as if the Nabateans wanted to play a trick on future generations. However, the structure must have had a specific function; its existence shows that archaeology must still resolve countless questions. This is part of what makes it so fascinating.

THE MUSEUMS

To the right of Kasr el Bint, close to the refreshment area set in the shade of some trees, an easily identified flight of large stone and concrete steps leads to the Old Museum, housed in a hypogeum dug in the side of al Habis. The terrace in front of the entrance – on which are arranged bas-reliefs, friezes and fragments of carvings – affords a splendid view of the valley below and the Royal Tombs. The original purpose of the three adjacent chambers (illuminated by large windows), which house the archaeological collections is the subject of conjecture. The rock complex was probably not a tomb but a temple. Beside the door there is a lovely headless statue of Hercules, found during the excavation of the theater; above the entrance is a magnificent bearded head, very possibly a Roman copy of a Greek original depicting Zeus. Inside (the extraordinary polychrome walls alone are worth a visit) are several carvings, pieces of friezes and festoons as well as bas-reliefs; most of this material is of Hellenistic inspiration although some

pieces are Roman copies or imported works. The high quality of execution demonstrates that the inhabitants of Petra – unique for the Nabatean kingdom – had absorbed cultural influence from the Greco-Roman west and loved to surround themselves with beautiful objects. The museum also houses pottery of typically Nabatean production, coins and other artifacts. Not far from the Old Museum, in a flat area near the point where Wadi

Turkamaniya joins Wadi Mousa and 250 yards from Kasr el Bint, a structure built in the nineties houses the New Museum and restaurant. The spacious and well-lit rooms display the most recent finds (including pottery, coins, gold jewelery, and semi-precious stones), some of the carved fragments and objects previously housed in the Old Museum, as well as a considerable number of finds discovered in the Petra area and, until a few years ago, kept in the Archaeological Museum in Amman.

87 top left This bas-relief, depicting a sphinx, is also housed in the Old Museum.

87 center This male bust should perhaps be identified as the god Serapis, and is situated above the door of the Old Museum.

87 top right Housed in a modern purpose-built building, the New Museum contains works of art and everyday objects – dating from various periods – found during the numerous archaeological digs conducted in Petra.

86 top The old Museum is set up in a hypogeum, consisting of three adjacent rooms, presumed to have been a temple. This hypothesis is supported by the fact that a sacred street starts from this area, cut in the side of the al Habis rock and leading to a "holy place" in the Wadi Siyagh valley.

86 center This winged head in sandstone is part of the collection of the Old Museum: Alien to Greco-Roman figurative languages, on the contrary it displays markedly Oriental facial characteristics. This is probably a local interpretation of the god Ermes.

86 bottom Along the comfortable flight of steps up to the Old Museum, this bas-relief bust has been placed in a circular cornice, and is thought to be the effigy of Zeus (Jupiter), the chief deity of the Greco-Roman pantheon. The Nabateans probably assimilated this god with Dusares.

86-87 On the terrace overlooking the Old Museum you can admire this sandstone panel, on which is carved in bas-relief a cupid between two facing winged lions. The fragment must have been part of a balustrade situated inside a temple.

88 top The Byzantine
church of Petra was a
building with three
aisles, supported by rows
of columns and
concluded to the east by
as many apses. In one of
these, the marble
balustrade adorned with
bas-relief crosses that
stood before the altar has
been reconstructed.

and walls must have been richly decorated with mosaics in polychrome tesserae of vitreous paste, regrettably nearly all lost. The floor of the nave, in slabs of marble with local sandstone inserts, is also greatly damaged but the mosaic floors of the two aisles were more fortunate and are only slightly damaged. These portray numerous figures, animals and symbols bound to Christian rites and subjects taken from classical tradition, enclosed in geometrical frames of various forms. Paradoxically, the ruin of the church has saved these splendid floors, as the layer of debris saved them from further damage by the elements and the fury of the iconoclasts, who disfigured many other mosaics in Jordan. Fragments of the altars and the marble transennas that stood before them have been found in the apse; one of these has been recomposed there. In December 1993 numerous ecclesiastical manuscript scrolls were found in a chamber adjacent to the church; although damaged by the fire that devastated the church, they are still legible.

89 *Of excellent workmanship, the floors of the two aisles date from the golden era of mosaic art in Jordan, which ideally began in 530 AD and ended in the first decades of the seventh century. Until the time of the discovery made in the Byzantine church of Petra, it was common opinion that*

the great tradition of mosaic had developed in Jordan mainly in the northernmost part of the country, in particular at Madaba and Gerasa. Although they have yet to be carefully analyzed, the mosaics of Petra are quite clearly the work of highly specialized artists, masters of a figurative lexicon extremely well evolved. Some subjects, such as the personification of Ocean recognizable at the bottom right, had not been identified before in any other mosaic of the same period in Jordan. Also of great interest is the rich repertoire of animal species in both aisles.

88 - 89 and 88 bottom The mosaics of Petra bear witness to the permanence, in the Christian-Byzantine cultural spheres, of iconographic elements taken from the classical world. It is no accident that the subjects of the pictures depict the Seasons, personified according to the stylistic features of Greco-Roman art.

North of the Colonnade Street and east of the temple of the Winged Lions stands a large tensile structure, visible for miles: This shelters the remains – still being studied and restored – of a large Christian church dating from the sixth century AD, the Byzantine period. At the time, Petra was the seat of the metropolitan bishop of the province of *Palaestina Tertia* and it is thus highly likely, also considering the size of the building and its rich decoration, that this was a cathedral. The monument was discovered in 1973 by the American archaeologist Kenneth Russell, but digging did not commence until May 1992 and has continued in subsequent years. From the very beginning it was clear that the church – with a basilica plan, three apses facing east and an atrium on the opposite side – was destroyed by fire and an earthquake shortly after its construction. The tremor was probably the disastrous one of 551, which shook much of Petra to the ground. Despite the collapse of most of the structures, archaeologists have been able to ascertain that the apses

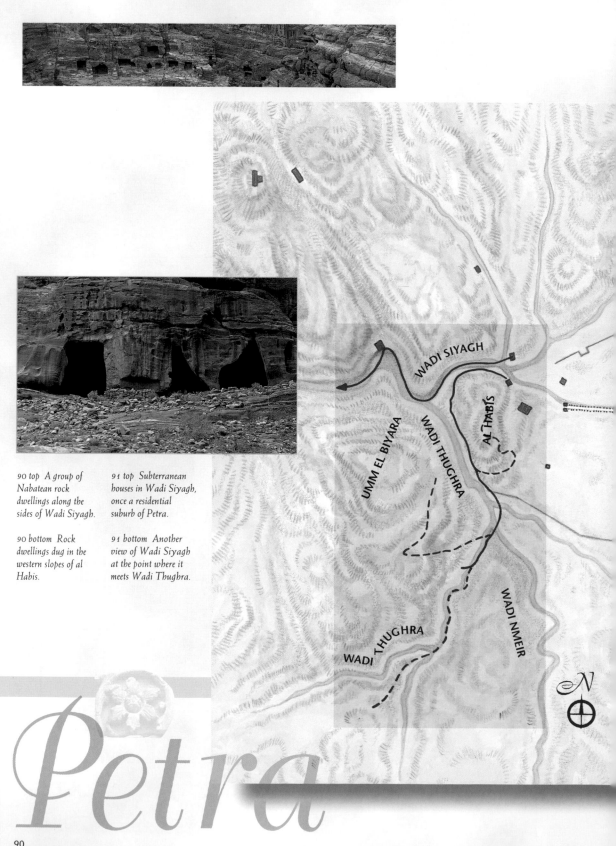

90 top A group of
Nabatean rock
dwellings along the
sides of Wadi Siyagh.

90 bottom Rock
dwellings dug in the
western slopes of al
Habis.

91 top Subterranean
houses in Wadi Siyagh,
once a residential
suburb of Petra.

91 bottom Another
view of Wadi Siyagh
at the point where it
meets Wadi Thughra.

WADI SIYAGH

AL HABIS

UMM EL BIYARA

WADI THUGHRA

WADI THUGHRA

WADI

WADI NMEIR

N

Petra

WADI SIYAGH AND WADI THUGHRA

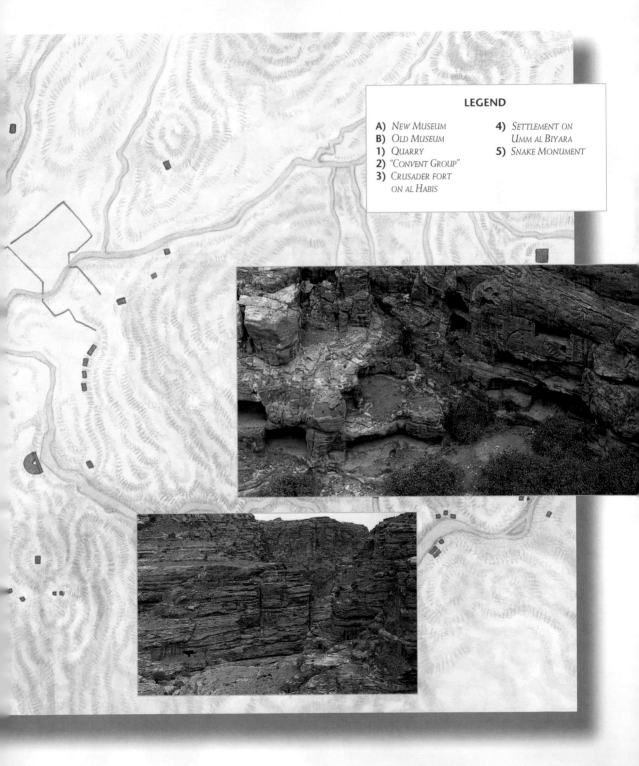

LEGEND

A) New Museum
B) Old Museum
1) Quarry
2) "Convent Group"
3) Crusader fort on al Habis

4) Settlement on Umm al Biyara
5) Snake Monument

WADI SIYAGH AND WADI THUGHRA

Interesting excursions can be made from the Old and New Museums into the Wadi Siyagh valley, where one of Petra's major suburbs used to lie, and along Wadi Thughra, to the so-called "Southern Graves." Those with more time can plan a visit in the same area to the top of al Habis or Umm el Biyara, but these are by no means easy excursions. Because no monuments of fundamental importance are situated there, these trips are recommended to

south, along the Wadi Thughra valley. Here the eye is immediately drawn to a Nabatean tomb preceded by a flower garden and a vegetable patch. This is the home of a very courteous Bedouin family and your presence should be discreet. Behind their unusual "house" is the fine pediment façade of a *triclinium*. Not far ahead, several feet below the level of the road, which here allows the passage of vehicles, is the so-called "Convent Group."

92 top This holy place is also dug in the rocky outcrop that juts out over Wadi Siyagh.

92 bottom The "Convent Group" would seem to have had a specific function, but the tombs may have simply been dug in a disused quarry.

those who are able to spend several days in Petra. A processional way dug into the side of al Habis departs from the terrace of the Old Museum and leads west; the route is quite frightening for several yards but is safe. This favorable spot affords splendid views of Wadi Siyagh down below and the point where Wadi Thughra flows into it from the southeast. For a few hundred feet all around the path, the rocks abound with channels, cisterns and holy sites. At a certain point the processional way turns sharply to the left and heads

This remarkable complex comprises a large square courtyard, dug at a depth of approximately 18 feet in a sandstone shelf. The walls are lined with tombs devoid of decoration, save for one with a simple cavetto façade. The overall appearance resembles that of a convent and hence the name. Access is down a flight of steps, from the south side; a second flight, on the north side and now badly eroded, used to descend to a larger courtyard, with a niche and a baetylus. On the rocky plateau that forms the west side of the

Convent Group is a holy area – or "place of sacrifice" – with the base of the altar on one side. Some believe that the processional way led here and that the Convent housed the priests responsible for the sacred duties. Visible from this spot, along the course of Wadi Siyagh, is the Nabatean quarry described below. If you return to the dirt road you will see it continues southward, along the sides of al Habis, skirting numerous tombs. By following this for a few hundred yards then bearing left again, you can go all the

92-93 and 93 bottom right A cavetto tomb situated along the processional way from the Old Museum to the Convent Group is still inhabited by a Bedouin family.

93 top The beautiful pediment façade of a triclinium is carved on the northwestern spur of el Habis. Visible just above it is a deep channel, along which flowed one of the many Nabatean aqueducts.

93 bottom right Only one of the chambers in the Convent Group has a cavetto façade; the others are totally devoid of decoration but were probably tombs nonetheless.

way around the mountain. Shortly before reaching the Columbarium you will see a flight of recently opened steps, the easiest way to climb to the top of al Habis. Here are the sparse remains of a crusader's fort, some Nabatean ruins and a place of sacrifice cut in the stone. Actually the true reward for climbing this far up is the splendid view over the Petra valley. Continuing along the road and then

breathtaking. The dirt road along Wadi Thughra continues south toward the so-called "Southern Graves" (where the Snake Monument and two Djin Blocks also stand), the Nabatean suburb of el Sabrah (not yet extensively explored) and Jebel Haroun, on the top of which is the white tomb of Aaron. The latter two are some distance away and it is essential to go in the company of a guide.

crossing the bed of the river, you will come to a group of tombs carved into the walls of Umm el Biyara. A gorge opens to the left of the great double cornice façade, marked by four pilaster strips, and a spectacular but difficult road cut in the rock leads to its top. To climb this you need good footwear, a water supply and, if possible, a local guide. Initially the path crosses a number of screes, before turning into a smooth ramp, once marked by an arch, which forms a bend. Farther on, the way becomes precipitous and rather dangerous. On the flat top of the mountain are some enormous cisterns and the partially excavated remains of several Edomite and Nabatean installations. Once more, the view is

of their homes and public buildings.

Approximately 500 yards ahead there is a perpetual spring, where the Wadi starts to become an ever-narrower gorge. All around, the rocks are dotted with the customary Nabatean channelling, religious niches and baetyli. One of these has stylized eyes and nose and an inscription identifying it as an effigy of Atargatis, the Syrian goddess of water and fertility. A few hundred yards on is the unexpected spectacle of a waterfall, but the way is by no means easy and indeed can be dangerous.

The Wadi Siyagh valley can also be visited from the New Museum, following the banks of the river. The gorge is dotted with rock dwellings, some of which still preserve part of the external walls and entrance steps. One of the subterranean houses is closed with a locked door (permission to enter must be obtained from the Department of Antiquities). The internal walls can be seen through the cracks in the door frame and are frescoed in brightly colored panels containing architectural perspectives. Nearby, at the end of a right-hand bend in the river, the side of the mountain seems to have been cut in a bizarre fashion. This is one of the quarries from which the Nabateans procured material for the construction

94 top right To the
rear of the picture is the
great Nabatean quarry
along Wadi Siyagh.

94 center right The
looming walls of Umm
al Biyara, in the Wadi
Thughra valley, are
dotted with tombs.

94 bottom right The
sides of a Djin Block in
the Southern Grave
area are carved with
Assyrian crow steps.

95 The so-called
"Southern Graves" are
dug in a light-colored
sandstone platform
between the courses of
Wadi Thughra and
Wadi Nmeir. One of
the most striking
structures in the
necropolis is this Djin
Block, called a "tower
tomb" by some, a temple
by others; it is the only
known two-story
monument of this type in
Petra. Carved on a
rocky spur not far away
is the Snake Monument,
a monolithic block –
much worn and not
particularly photogenic
– which can be
identified as a coiled
reptile. It may be an
apotropaic symbol or
the symbolic effigy of
the god Dusares... or
something else
completely.

96 top *The Lion Triclinium, one of the most elegant examples of a pediment façade.*

96 bottom *A detail of the façade of the Deir, the most important monument in Petra.*

97 top *A sweeping view of the Deir, preceded by a deep courtyard.*

97 bottom *The processional way that leads to the Deir passes through landscapes of untamed beauty.*

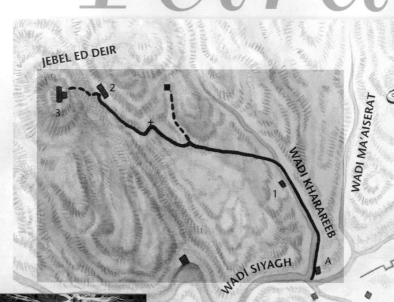

JEBEL ED DEIR

WADI KHARAREEB

WADI MA'AISERAT

WADI SIYAGH

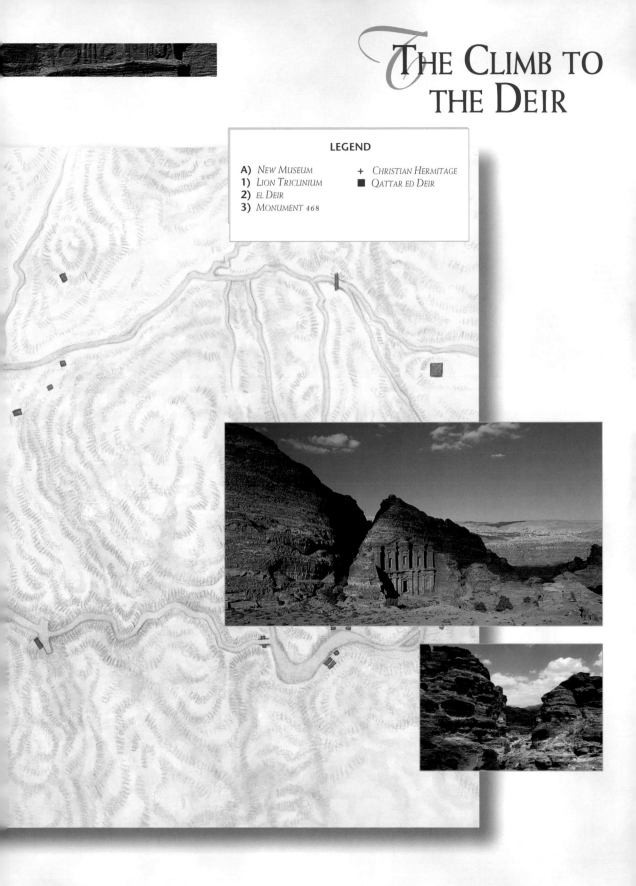

LEGEND

A) NEW MUSEUM
1) LION TRICLINIUM
2) EL DEIR
3) MONUMENT 468

+ CHRISTIAN HERMITAGE
■ QATTAR ED DEIR

98 and 99 top A bridge
originally stood before the
Lion Triclinium, providing
access to its chamber up a
flight of steps. The wind
has eroded the rock
between the doorway and
the oculus above it,
creating an unusual
"keyhole" aperture.

THE ASCENT TO THE DEIR

Winding through the ruins of
Petra, a visit to the Deir is one of the
loveliest here. This excursion is a
must, not just because it visits one
of antiquity's most spectacular
monuments, but also for the
untamed beauty of the surrounding
scenery. The route may be rather
long and involves a considerable
climb, but the path is easy to follow.
We do recommend against
commencing the hike in late
morning, to avoid exposure to the
burning sun on the steepest section.
The path starts in front of the New
Museum and is marked.
The path runs northwest from the
New Museum along the bed of a
stream called Wadi Kharareeb.

THE LION TRICLINIUM

Surrounded on both sides by rock
structures, the valley gradually narrows
and the track comes to a fork, half-
concealed in the bushes. The path to
the left leads, in a very short time, to
the Lion Triclinium. Often erroneously
identified as a tomb, this is of
considerable interest because it is one
of the few underground triclinia to
have survived intact. Dug into the head
of the small wadi, beside a crack that
turns into a waterfall in the rainy

season, the façade is much eroded, but
still comprehensible. Pedimented in
type, it stands between two half-pillars
with engaged quarter columns and
capitals with vegetable motifs. The badly
damaged portal is flanked by the two
figures of lions in bas-relief that gave
the monument its name. The entablature
is decorated with a Doric frieze, in
which triglyphs alternate with *paterae*.
Carved at the ends are two Medusa
heads. The pediment, its *tympanum*
decorated with foliage, supports an
acroterion in the form of an urn.

99 bottom left The left
wall of the Lion
Triclinium has a niche
containing a baetylus
dedicated to Dusares
and two tombs (one
of which is seen in
the photograph).
The presence of these
burial places explains
the existence of the
triclinium, needed for
the funeral rites held in
honor of the dead.

99 right Because of the
refined decorations
developed over the façade
of the triclinium (this
function being confirmed
by the presence inside of
a triclinial bed) the
monument has been
ascribed to the rule of
Aretas IV (8 BC-40
AD). Others, however,
believe it dates from the
Roman period. Lions
were sacred to the
goddess Al Uzza.

THE PROCESSIONAL WAY AND THE CHRISTIAN HERMITAGE

To proceed towards the Deir from the Lion Triclinium, first return to the main path, which from the fork, becomes gradually steeper. After veering to the west along the gorge excavated by the Wadi al Deir, the sandy trail very soon turns into what used to be a processional way, hewn into the rock at numerous points. To reach your destination you must be prepared to climb more than 800 steps and follow sections cut into the side of the cliffs, but the natural scenery, the incredible colors of the sandstone and the scenic spots that follow one after the other justify the effort. Besides the natural beauty, along the way you can also admire some interesting monuments. Where the path enters Wadi al Deir – on the wall to the

100-101 Petra is not only rock tombs and temples, as nature quite rightly also plays a leading role – for the monuments carved by man would lose much of their charm without these amazing settings.

100 top *The climb along the ancient processional way from Petra to the Deir takes approximately an hour and passes through scenery of unequalled beauty. All around you, fine sandstone walls streaked with multicolored veining are a delirium of surreal forms that have been shaped by erosion.*

101 left *An amazing staircase carved in a zigzag is visible right opposite the Christian hermitage, on a knoll of light-colored sandstone. Impossible to climb now because the first flight is so badly worn, this once led to cisterns supplied by a complex system of channels.*

101 right *Steps, steps and more steps. Those wishing to admire the grandest monument in Petra have to accept some hardship, although the processional way also affords no lack of delights: banks of rock in the most incredible colors, stunning views and even a passage below a huge boulder.*

100 bottom *The so-called "Christian hermitage" is situated in a spectacular position not far from the Deir. Christian symbols have been found carved inside the main chamber, very probably a Nabatean hypogeum adapted for a different use in the Byzantine period.*

right, as you climb – you will see a tympanum façade, the highly eroded door of which is framed between two characteristic Nabatean half-pillars. The two benches inside suggest this was not a tomb but a *biclinium* and the loculus dug in the floor dates from a far later era. Three-quarters of the way towards your destination, a turn to the right will lead the more curious up a side valley to Qattar al Deir, a rock balcony near a huge cistern that is supplied by underground springs and remains full all year round. This is yet another eloquent example of the remarkable water reserves accumulated by the Nabateans.

Continuing along the processional way, after a fairly steep section full of bends and flights of steps, you reach a white sandstone promontory which affords a splendid view of the Royal Tombs and the surrounding valleys. To the left opens a deep gorge, wedged between sheer walls, which meets up with Wadi Siyagh. To the right towers a pinnacle of rock with some artificial cavities. One of these doors leads to a semi-hypogean chamber extending out into the void, the external masonry wall of which has partially collapsed; the other entrance leads to a room with crosses and other Christological symbols carved into the back wall. This is thought to have been a Christian hermitage in the Byzantine period. At its foot, the way continues along the edge of the chasm before starting to climb again.

THE DEIR

The Deir is visible from some distance away, when the gigantic urn that decorates the top of the *tholos* appears suddenly from behind a curtain of rocks. The contrast between this perfectly geometric form and the incoherent mass of eroded sandstone that surrounds it, is truly surreal. A last flight of steps, enclosed between high pinnacles, dotted with oleanders and junipers, and the processional way comes to an end, in a saddle at the foot of Jebel al Deir, the mountain that dominates the Petra valley to the west. The monument's façade is set a good few feet back from the side of the mountain, so that it is not seen until the last minute. The emotional impact produced by the appearance of this superb construction is unforgettable. The Deir stands out against the rocky ridge behind it as if recently freed from the embrace of the natural matter. Virtually intact, spared from the fury of

102-103 The Deir is perhaps the Nabatean architects' most astounding and grandiose creation. The façade of this huge construction seems to come forth from the rock, as if proudly asserting the victory of human genius over natural matter.

102 bottom Certainly the most impressive monument in Petra, the Deir stands in an isolated position on the top of a mountain spur. The photograph shows the enormous and mysterious round clearing that lies just a short distance from the rock construction.

the elements that almost destroyed other monuments in Petra, it seems superhuman in the purity of its design. You are overwhelmed by its size, which is extraordinary: The front measures 160 feet wide by 127 feet high. Although situated in a less spectacular position than the Khasneh, the Deir looks even more impressive and the simple decoration adds to its austere majesty. Few other monuments in the world – save for Abu Simbel – possess similar charm.

The front of the building is divided into two stories. The lower one, marked at the corners by two semi-pillars with the customary engaged quarter columns, has six tall half-columns crowned with Nabatean capitals. The central intercolumn contains the pedimented

103 top The Deir's dimensions are extraordinary. The conical roof of the central tholos crowned with an urn on a Nabatean capital, is 30 feet high and the doorway is 26 feet high.

doorway, once preceded by a flight of constructed steps, whereas the external intercolumns have two deep rectangular niches, each crowned with a semi-circular tympanum. A high broken entablature, devoid of ornament, supports the second story, carved in very high relief out of the mountainside. The large central *tholos*, with a conical roof and crowned with an urn, is enclosed at the sides by two semi-pediments. The *tholos* and semi-pediments are supported on half-columns with Nabatean "horn" capitals and, in the intercolumns, present deep rectangular niches. Like those on the lower story, these must have housed statues. The whole is closed, at the ends, by two avant-corps, each marked by a half-pillar with a quarter column leaning on the inner side. The half-pillars and half-columns on the upper floor are aligned with those below. A long, very elegant, Doric frieze in which the metopes are replaced by very low-relieved disks links the various architectural elements of the second floor with each other. Not surprisingly, compared with the magnificence of the façade, the interior appears strikingly bare. It consists of a huge almost cubic

chamber, 36 feet square, without ornament. Only in the back wall is there a large arcosolium niche, flanked by half-pillars, the stucco frame of which suggests that the whole chamber was originally plastered and painted. At the center, raised above the floor and reached via two flights of steps on the sides, is a sort of altar, or platform. The foundations of two benches have recently been found along the walls of the room, half-buried in the debris. Their presence would suggest that the

103 bottom A disquieting, titanic creature produced out of the solid rock, the Deir stands on a rise isolated from the rest of the city, solitary as only a monarch can and must be.

104 top The huge doorway of the Deir leads to a large chamber approximately 36 feet square, devoid of ornament save for the arcosolium niche dug in the back wall. Several Christian crosses carved inside (now difficult to see) bear witness to the fact that the mausoleum was used in the Byzantine period as a church or perhaps a monks' refuge. Indeed, the Arab name for the building, al Deir, means "the Monastery."

104-105 The façade of the Deir is set deeply in the mountain and was preceded by a large courtyard made by excavating the rock for a distance of approximately 200 feet in front of it. For an idea of the true size of the monument, suffice to think that the temple of Abu Simbel, in Nubia, is 125 feet wide and 101 high. As it is a monolith, the Deir — and all the other rock structures in Petra — should be thought of more as a huge piece of sculpture than as a building.

Deir was used as a *biclinium* or a *heroon*, a mausoleum constructed to commemorate the figure of a deified monarch. The great room would thus have served for ceremonies and symposia. It is common theory that the mausoleum was consecrated to king Obodas I (96-86 BC), who died at Advat, a Nabatean city in the Negev Desert. This assumption is supported by the presence, on a rocky wall not far from the Deir, of an inscription naming Obodas and mentioning a confraternity set up in his honor. On the basis of these considerations, the monument should date from the first century BC, and thus be the same age as the Khasneh. The appearance of the building would, however, seem to contradict this theory. Often people have stressed the similarity between the Deir and the Khasneh, but it is a matter of impression rather than of substance. Firstly, in the Deir the height and width ratio is inverted compared with that of the "Treasury"; secondly, the pronaos of the Khasneh rests on free-standing columns, which lead to a deep vestibule, whereas here there is only the slightest suggestion of a portico. Lastly, the decoration of the Deir is totally untouched by the Greek influence so obvious in the Khasneh; the capitals are

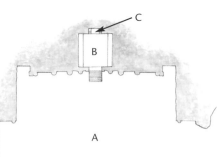

A COURTYARD
B CHAMBER
C ARCOSOLIUM
NICHE

typically Nabatean and even the Doric frieze looks like a local interpretation. It could be said that the builders of the Deir set out to intentionally assert their independence from the languages of Alexandria and the Greek world in general. The play of voids and solids, the rhythmic alternation of straight and curved lines, the chiaroscuro effect produced by the broken line of the entablature between the two stories, the convex line of the *tholos* contrasted with the concave one of the exedra of the lower story, which contains the portal,

his people to their ancient splendor, rejecting all links with foreign influences.

In the absence of concrete evidence, the matter remains open to debate. Another element still to be investigated is the presence of the huge courtyard in front of the building, usually hastily defined as an area used for mass holy ceremonies. Interestingly, however, both the rocky slopes bordering the courtyard were clearly levelled at the edges and two pilaster strips (see the plan here and the drawing on the next pages) on the two walls thus obtained were spared. Moreover, the debris half-buried in the sand, 30 yards from the façade reveals several column drums, some still covered with a thick layer of fluted stuccowork. It is therefore possible that a raised block stood before the building, a colonnaded portico surrounding a sort of *temenos*. This too is, at present, mere supposition.

all give the monument a great sense of modernity. It almost appears that, overcoming the conventions of Hellenistic art, the Nabatean builders managed to anticipate Baroque style. It is therefore more likely that the Deir was indeed conceived as a heroon in Obodas I's honor, but long after his death and, more precisely, during the reign of the last Nabatean king, Rabbel II (70-106 AD), who set out to return

105 The bell-shaped roof of the tholos is reached up a flight of steps carved in the sandstone, to the right of the façade of the Deir. In the back of the picture, to the right, is the huge cavity known as Room or Monument 468, which contains the finest and best-preserved religious aedicula in Petra.

106-107 This hypothetical reconstruction shows a colonnaded portico in front of the Deir that marks a vast holy area or a temenos, in which the followers of the confraternity honoring Obodas celebrated their rites. Some writers (including Bachmann) have already presumed the existence of enclosed spaces in front of some of Petra's rock structures; the Tomb of Uneishu and the Roman Soldier Tomb are the most obvious examples. If this is so, the substructures in front of the Urn Tomb may originally have supported a colonnaded block that was the continuation of the two porticoes dug in the rock in the front of the building. These enclosures seem most commonly associated with triclinia or at least with tombs having such chambers. It is above all true that both triclinia and enclosures were essential to carry out funeral and convivial rites. This would confirm the function of the Deir as a cenotaph of the deified king Obodas, because its sole chamber was indeed a biclinium.

The area around the Deir has been little explored and, consequently, little studied. Yet, it is full of very interesting remains. The rock wall to the left of the great rock sanctuary is lined with water channels, cisterns, hypogeums and religious niches. A bas-relief group portraying two figures leading a dromedary, situated at the entrance to a side gorge, resembles the similar group recently discovered in the Interior Siq. Almost in front of the Deir, in a slightly raised position, is a huge circular clearing, partly obtained by excavating the rock and partly marked by a low wall, now half destroyed.

The function of this area, whether as *temenos*, open-air sanctuary or place of sacrifice, is completely unknown. At the northeastern end of the hill where the Deir stands, a heap of almost incomprehensible ruins is perhaps all that remains of a temple or a *tholos*. Nonetheless, the most interesting monument – number 468 in Brünnow's classification – is carved in the striking rocky hummock that stands just over 500 yards as the crow

108 bottom left
The aedicula *inside Monument 468 is splendidly preserved and consists of a niche – which must have contained the statue of a deity – crowned with an entablature and Doric frieze, framed between two pilaster strips supporting a second entablature with two busts at the ends. Obviously of Hellenistic influence, the whole is topped with a pediment and three acroteria.*

flies in front of the Deir.

Today it is a vast square cavity, totally devoid of a façade, its sole interest lying in the splendid tympanum niche dug in the back wall. This chamber must have been the cell of an enormous religious building – perhaps the most impressive in Petra – razed by one of the numerous earthquakes that have struck the region in the past. As you approach the rock you will notice that the terrace in front of the room is artificial, once reached up one or two monumental flights of steps; this substructure very probably supported a gigantic pronaos comprising 10 or 12 columns in front, the bases of which are still visible.

The whole appearance of the mountain was very different in the past. If you climb to the top – extremely carefully — you will see a sweeping section of Wadi Arabah and the Deir, but you will also see large sections of wall, the basement of a small *tholos* (or a circular chamber at

108 top right In front of the Deir in the map drawn by Laborde is the plan of Monument 468, with a large pronaos in front of it. David Roberts (see the drawing on pages 32-33) also noticed the remains of the building and drew the bases of the columns.

108 bottom right This photograph, taken in spring 1998 on the top of the rock in which Monument 468 is dug, shows the bases of some half-columns that were part of a circular chamber.

109 top left The left wall of the Deir is filled with aedicula and votive niches, an indication that the hill at the foot of Jebel al Deir was considered a particularly sacred place.

109 top right Erosion has produced a bizarre shape in a tomb near the Deir.

least) and even the remains of a mosaic floor in black and white tesserae. Clearly, Monument 468 and the structures above it must have been part of a monumental complex of considerable importance, especially given its raised position overlooking the saddle of Jebel al Deir and its monuments. It is known that the Nabateans liked to erect their holiest sanctuaries on the tops of mountains. When and to whom the complex was consecrated are mysteries still to be investigated.

109 center It is very hard to imagine what Monument 468 and the structures above it must have looked like, although it was certainly an architectural complex of considerable size.

109 bottom In the vicinity of the Deir are some platforms cut into the rock, usually adjacent to small basins. These places must have been used to hold offertorial ceremonies.

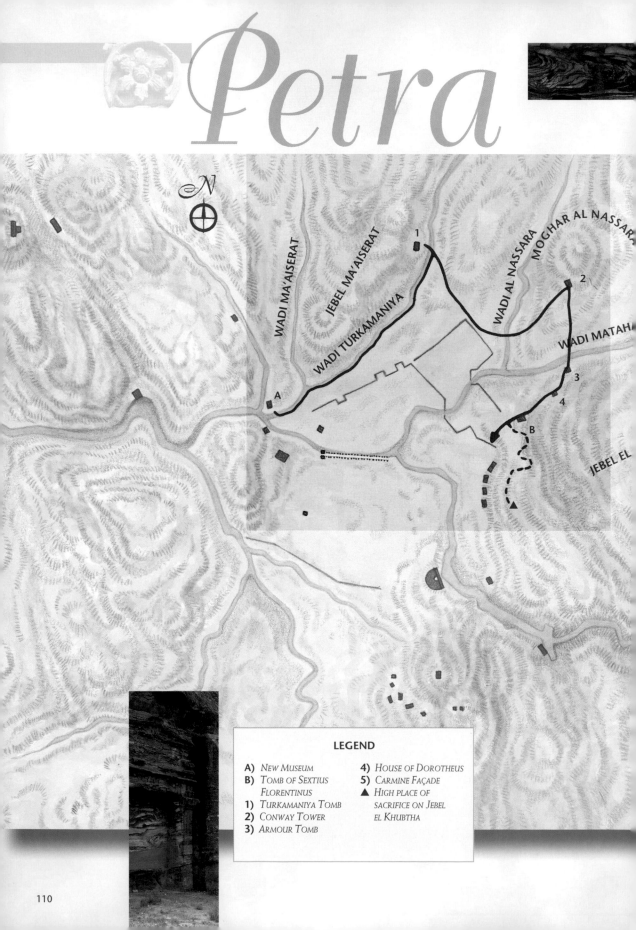

Petra

N

WADI MA'AISERAT

JEBEL MA'AISERAT

WADI TURKAMANIYA

WADI AL NASSARA

MOGHAR AL NASSARA

WADI MATAH

JEBEL EL

1

2

3

4

A

B

LEGEND

A) *New Museum*
B) *Tomb of Sextius Florentinus*
1) *Turkamaniya Tomb*
2) *Conway Tower*
3) *Armour Tomb*

4) *House of Dorotheus*
5) *Carmine Façade*
▲ *High place of sacrifice on Jebel el Khubtha*

KHUBTHA

110 bottom The Carmine Façade is carved on the northern slopes of Jebel el Khubtha; its function is unknown.

110-111 The rocks of Jebel el Khubtha feature particularly bright colours; the shades are produced by the different chemical composition of the various layers of sandstone.

111 top Numerous niches and other rock structures with distinctive bright colourings are scattered within a hundred feet or so around the Carmine Façade.

111 bottom The spectacular rock-carved flight of steps that leads to the holy place on Jebel el Khubtha provides picturesque views.

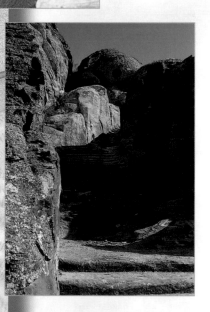

THE TURKAMANIYA TOMB

The itinerary proposed here is quite long but can be divided into small sections, according to the time available and specific personal interests; it does cover three areas that differ greatly from one another. The monuments visited, although not of primary importance, are very interesting. For logistical reasons you are advised to start the excursion from the New Museum, climbing to the northeast along the dirt track that skirts the bed of Wadi Turkamaniya. This pleasantly green valley has a plentiful water supply and was already farmed in Nabatean times. On both sides the rock slopes are studded with tombs and places of sacrifice. After twenty minutes or so, you will come to a tomb that is easily recognized, as it has lost the whole bottom half of its façade, swept away over the centuries by violent river floods. This is the Turkamaniya Tomb, also known as the Tomb with the Nabatean Inscription.

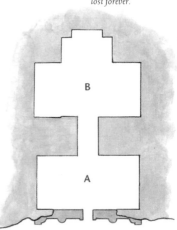

A *VESTIBULE*
B *FUNERARY CHAMBER*

The darker area shows the parts of the façade lost forever.

112 top The lovely façade of the Turkamaniya Tomb was seriously damaged by the violent flooding of the nearby wadi (Who the Turkman who gave his name to the tomb and the valley was remains

one of Petra's many mysteries). Soon, a major restoration operation will consolidate the structure and make the important Nabatean inscription safe from any further damage.

Deemed one of the most elegant examples of the double-cornice façade, the front is divided by two half-columns and two lateral half-pillars with engaged quarter columns. The sub-attic is divided by four short pilaster strips, in line with the half-columns and, like these, crowned with Nabatean capitals. The main reason for its interest, however, is the long inscription carved in the central intercolumn above the door at a height of more than 20 feet. Although it does not bear the name of the owner of the tomb, nor mention any king, the style of writing dates the

monument to the reign of Malchus II (40-70 AD). It contains a formula that was used to place the tomb and all its ancillaries under the eternal protection of Dusares. The inscription is of fundamental importance because the first part lists all the structures that evidently formed an integral part of the tomb of a wealthy person: a porticoed courtyard, a triclinium, gardens, wells and other ancillary chambers. Clearly the vast majority of Petra's tombs that have survived to the present day are missing their constructed parts, razed by earthquakes and floods.

112 center left and bottom right The Nabatean language is classified in the Aramaic group. Unfortunately no literary works have survived, only rock inscriptions. That adorning the façade of the Turkamaniya Tomb is the only one of some length found in Petra. It states that the tomb and all its ancillaries are under the protection of the god Dusares and that "no one else except him who has in writing

a contract" may be buried here. This privilege was usually extended to the owner's children and closest relatives.

MOGHAR AL NASSARA AND THE ARMOR TOMB

112-113 The photograph shows the central part of Moghar al Nassara. The Armor Tomb is clearly visible to the left.

113 top right A vast necropolis lies among the rocks of Jebel Ma'aiserat, to the east of Wadi Turkamaniya. Numerous interesting structures surround this double-cornice tomb.

After the Turkamaniya Tomb, those with a few hours to spare can explore the tombs that stud the slopes of Jebel Ma'aiserat above, on the left side of Wadi Turkamaniya. There is a complete range of Nabatean architectural models: well-conserved tombs, holy ways and courtyards dug in the rock, sanctuaries and "places of sacrifice" where lambs were offered to the gods. The area is lovely but extremely vast and it is advisable to carry a good supply of water with you. If, on the other hand, you wish to reach the Moghar al Nassara necropolis, leave the Turkamaniya

purpose. Walk northeast from the Conway Tower and cross the bed of Wadi Nassara to eventually reach the Moghar al Nassara heights. This major suburb of Petra, which for some inexplicable reason was never included within the ring of walls, was named for the numerous crosses carved in the hypogea, probably during the Byzantine period. "Nassara" means "Nazarene," the term used by the Arabs for the Christians. There are all kinds of tombs in this area, but the most famous is the Armor Tomb. Facing south, this has a lovely double cornice with a sub-attic divided by four short pilaster strips and crowned with Nabatean capitals. In the spaces between these are carved two Medusa heads and trophies; one depicts the armor which gave the monument its name. This highly unusual frieze is unique in Nabatean architecture.

113 bottom right The Armor Tomb — actually it might have been a triclinium, probably preceded by the customary porticoed courtyard — is famous for the unusual frieze that adorns the sub-attic. This monument may date from the second half of the first century AD.

113 center right The Moghar al Nassara ridge is full of rock structures — from the oldest pit tombs to some examples of the so-called "Nabatean Classical style." On the west side of the rock is a section of the old road that climbed to the suburb of el Barid; a "place of sacrifice" is situated in the northernmost area.

Tomb and cross the bed of the *wadi*, then head southeast. After hiking approximately 20 minutes, you will notice the clearly visible remains of the Nabatean ring of walls, built to defend Petra's northern districts. The area overlooking the walls is occupied by the partially explored Turkamaniya Necropolis. In the northwest corner of the wall stand the massive foundations of a round tower, known as the Conway Tower, named after the archaeologist who commenced the excavations in 1929. Approximately six feet thick, the wall was built around a projecting rock, and evidence suggests that it was built for a defensive

THE WADI MATAHA AND THE HOUSE OF DOROTHEUS

The large Moghar al Nassara ridge is bordered to the southeast by the course of Wadi Mataha; the waters of Wadi Mousa, diverted at the mouth of the Siq, flow into this wadi. It is quite easy to descend to the bed of the river from the Armor Tomb, but you must beware of the pit graves dug in the banks of sandstone. The panorama is particularly agreeable; growing amidst rocks in surreal colors and shapes are thick oleander bushes; in the hottest hours of the day the air is filled with their fragrance. This slope is also studded with façades, most of the "cavetto" or "double cornice" type. Opposite rises the great rock wall of Jebel el Khubtha, at the bottom perforated with a myriad of shady apertures; above this runs the straight

114 right The House of Dorotheus, as well as the other rock dwellings dug in the slopes of Jebel el Khubtha, is reached via daring flights of steps and rather vertiginous passages and must be approached with great care.

114-115 The House of Dorotheus consists of about 20 connecting rooms. This was probably the home of a wealthy man and his family. The Nabatean aqueduct is also visible in the photograph.

114 top left Some of the chambers that make up the so-called "House of Dorotheus" are illuminated by large windows on two stories – their similarity with modern buildings is disconcerting.

114 bottom left The entrances of some rooms are flanked by one or more windows and preceded by a terrace; the stone is so worn that it is difficult to know whether the façades had any architectural decorations.

line of an aqueduct, like a thin wound cut in the side of the mountain. As can be gathered from their appearance, most of the hypogea were used as dwellings as this must have been a heavily populated suburb of Petra. The rock face is in the shade for much of the day and the area is rich in water, so living conditions were particularly good.

A complex of connecting chambers, reached via a steep flight of steps, is known as the House of Dorotheus, after two Greek inscriptions mentioning this name found on the inside walls. Here, as everywhere else in the area, erosion and earthquakes have seriously damaged the rock houses but you can still picture what this unusual district looked like: well-plastered façades, terraces and flights of steps flanked by wooden parapets, roof and vegetable gardens kept lush by the water collected in the large cisterns, the course of the *wadi* closed between strong embankments and a good road descending to the center of the metropolis. The river was crossed by masonry bridges and fields and meadows lined the shores. Although conditions have changed since then, some still appreciate the Nabatean residences, and Bedouin families continue to occupy hypogea in the western part of the valley. Several families belonging to the Bdoul and Liyatheneh tribes reside on Petra's archaeological site. They are the modern-day inhabitants of the Rose-red City. The government has built them modern homes near Wadi Mousa, but they seem to prefer their traditional lifestyle, living off shepherding and small-scale trading. They are proud, reserved, courteous and the elderly are slightly xenophobic. Please respect their privacy.

116 The rock face around the Carmine Façade, as well as the entire western side of Jebel el Khubtha, is literally studded with tombs, votive niches, rock dwellings, cisterns and channels. This area is a true paradise for trekking enthusiasts: there are miles upon miles of paths and steps carved into the rock which often lead to outstandingly scenic spots. It must, however, be remembered that many routes are eroded and in poor condition, others end abruptly in thin air (literally, on frightening overhangs), and others disappear into great expanses of rock where orientation becomes rather difficult. Those who are not accustomed to the mountains or to long difficult hikes, should keep to the main paths, because a wrong turn could have serious consequences.

Along the course of Wadi Mataha on the way towards the old inhabited center, not far past the House of Dorotheus, stands the structure known as the Carmine Façade. It is not easy to find at first, as it is dug in a recess in the rock wall and blocked by a thicket of oleander bushes. As in the case of the Silk Tomb, this mysterious monument is of interest for the bright coloring of the rock it is carved in. Of the pediment type and adorned with a Doric frieze, the façade has lost its door; hence the function of the structure is unknown. Approximately 200 yards farther ahead is the Tomb of Sextius Florentinus. From here it is easy to reach Colonnade Street and the New Museum, or return to Wadi Mousa along the Siq. A fascinating alternative for the hardier hikers is the spectacular processional way, which starts right behind the tomb enclosed between the walls of a narrow *wadi* where some Nabatean metalworkers must have once had their workshops. Entirely dug in the rock, the path passes beneath an arch (thought to have originally had two heavy wooden doors) before becoming a treacherous flight of steps. It ends on the flat top of Jebel el Khubtha where an important "place of sacrifice", a reservoir, partially covered with a vault, and the remains of other installations stand.

117 left Its colored veining makes the Carmine Façade an ideal subject for photographers, but it remains a mystery to archaeologists. It is unlikely to be an unfinished tomb or triclinium, because the chambers were dug before the architectural decoration was completed. Given its size it could hardly have been a votive niche either.

117 right Although the place of sacrifice and the other remains on Jebel el Khubtha are of some interest, the holy way that leads to them is far more spectacular. Once at the top of the mountain, walk south to a point that commands a breathtaking view of the façade of the Khasneh below. This area is home to an unusual bright blue lizard, the Agama sinaita.

Petra

WADI FARASA

JEBEL ATTUF

LEGEND

A) OUTER SIQ
B) TOMB OF UNEISHU
C) THEATRE
1) HIGH PLACE OF SACRIFICE
2) OBELISKS
3) LION MONUMENT
4) GARDEN TOMB
5) ROMAN SOLDIER TOMB
6) TRICLINIUM
7) RENAISSANCE TOMB
8) BROKEN PEDIMENT TOMB

119 top The Broken Pediment Tomb, an austere example of "Nabatean Classical Style".

119 bottom The portal of the Renaissance Tomb, crowned with an unusual segmental open pediment.

118 top A sweeping view of the Roman Soldier Tomb; in the foreground, to the left, is a large triclinial chamber.

118 bottom Detail of the façade of the Roman Soldier Tomb showing the three bas-reliefs that adorn the niches.

THE ASCENT OF JEBEL ATTUF

The ascent to the top of Jebel Attuf is perhaps the most demanding and tiring of those proposed in this book, but it is of fundamental interest for several reasons: first, because as well as visiting the Holy Place it also passes some of the most fascinating rock constructions in the area; secondly, because the route offers spectacular sweeping views of the Petra valley and surrounding mountains. This excursion should not be missed. As it takes at least three hours it is preferable to set off in the morning, to avoid walking in the hottest part of the day, although the view from the top of Jebel Attuf at sunset is breathtaking to say the least. Expert hikers can start the climb in the late afternoon and descend before the archaeological site closes. The best route is that on the Outer Siq side; the sanctuary on Jebel Attuf can also be reached from the Wadi Farasa valley,

but in this case you may have difficulty finding the right path. The holy way that commences just past Tomb 70, on the left side of the Siq, is well marked. The starting point for the ascent is unmistakable, immediately appearing as a never-ending flight of steps; in parts these become ramps, also carved in the rock. Looking to the left, you will see how the mountain was literally carved to pieces by the Nabateans. A double row of square niches (similar to those seen at the sides of the Khasneh) carved on the quarry face led the way to the higher terrace: a truly amazing, absolutely vertical flight of steps. You then follow a narrow valley, closed between sheer rock walls.

The processional way emerges

THE OBELISKS

abruptly in a saddle, a crack between two spurs dominated by two unusual obelisks that are visible from some distance. The top of Jebel Attuf, the highest point of which is 3,414 feet, is actually divided in two: the northern part is known as the "High place of sacrifice" (or Jebel Madhbah), the southern one as the "Obelisk ridge." Slightly less than 23 feet tall and 30 yards from each other, the two monuments stand isolated on a level area created by excavating the top of the mountain. These monoliths are commonly thought to represent Dusares and Al Uzza, but there is no conclusive evidence for this theory.

From the obelisk area it is possible,

THE HIGH PLACE

on the northern side of Jebel Madhbah, to observe the remains of strong walls and towers constructed on the edge of high, artificially squared rock faces. These walls are thought to be what remains of a crusader fort, probably erected on older foundations or possibly on the site of a Nabatean quarry. The path to the "High Place of Sacrifice" passes straight through the ruins before veering left, onto the bare rock. The objective is a hundred yards or so ahead, on the highest point of the mountain. The open-air sanctuary – preceded by a large cistern cut in the rock plateau – occupies a fairly small area, but is the best preserved of all those situated on the peaks around

120-121 Their appearance and the Arab name they are known by (Zibb Attuf, or "Merciful Phallus") suggest that the two obelisks may have been symbols of fertility or divinity linked to the concept of mercy.

A COURTYARD
B MENSA SACRA
C ALTAR
D LUSTRAL BASIN
E CISTERN

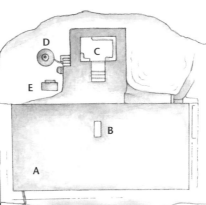

121 top The subject of this photograph is the large round basin situated to the left of the altar; the priests perhaps used it to collect the blood of the sacrificed lambs, which was then sprinkled all over the holy area.

121 Top This large water tank, just over three feet deep, is nine yards south of the courtyard and cut into the stone. It probably held the water required for the holy ceremonies.

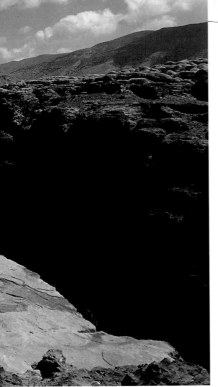

preceded by three steps, is situated right in front of the offerings table in a recess dug in the sandstone on the west side of the courtyard. On the top is a square hole, into which the baetylus symbolizing the divinity was almost certainly inserted. To the left of the altar is a large circular basin, approached up four steps, with a drain that discharged onto the steps. This may have been a basin where the blood of the victims sacrificed to the gods was collected, or where the priests washed after the ceremonies. The adjacent rectangular water tank perhaps contained pure water for the cleansing of the vessels used during the ceremonies. In ancient times the offering of blood to the gods bore great symbolic significance because blood was the symbol of life. Rites involving blood strengthened the bond between the gods and humans.

121 bottom The "High place of sacrifice" could not accommodate great masses of worshippers, a characteristic common to all the open-air holy places around Petra.

Unfortunately very little reliable evidence has survived as to the Nabatean religious practices, which in many ways resembled those of the Jews.

Petra. Given its position, so exposed to the elements, it seems incredible that it has not been totally eroded and that in many parts the rock seems only recently cut. The "High place of sacrifice" is a rectangular courtyard approximately 48 feet by 21 feet, surrounded by a low step that perhaps served as seating for those participating in the holy rites. In the middle of this perfectly levelled area is a platform, also rectangular, just six inches high. This is the "Mensa Sacra," where non-blood offerings to the gods – food, drink, stalks of wheat and perhaps also precious objects – were placed. The single block altar, approximately three feet high and

122 top right Along
the path that descends
from Jebel Attuf into
Wadi Farasa are
numerous dedicatory
inscriptions in the
Nabatean language;
this one, fronted by a
level area, is just a few
minutes from the top.

THE LION MONUMENT

The view over the Petra valley
from the "High place of sacrifice"
and indeed from the entire Jebel Madhbah
plateau is stunning. To the west is the
towering mass of Umm el Biyara and,
to the south, you can see Aaron's
Tomb, gleaming white on the top of
Jebel Haroun. It seems impossible to
descend to the west into the Wadi
Farasa valley from here, but simply

return to the obelisks, walk south for
a hundred yards or so and then turn
right, where an unexpected path – or
rather, a holy way – starts to wind
across the rock wall. Along the path
you will see numerous inscriptions
left by Nabatean pilgrims, a few
baetyli, and some of the most
spectacular color combinations in the
entire region. On the sides of a rocky
outcrop, to the right, is a rectangular
baetylus, crowned with a medallion
and bust. A few hundred yards past
this stands the Lion Monument.
Actually, this must have been a
fountain, judging from the remains of
channelling found. The now-headless
animal is 15 feet long and eight feet
tall.

122 top left Minus its
head (which was perhaps
in bronze) and so eroded
it looks like an elephant,
the Lion Monument was
a fountain with water
gushing from the animal's
mouth. The lion was an
animal sacred to the
goddess Al Uzza.

122 bottom left It is very
hard to interpret with
certainty the bust that
tops this baetylus cut in a
rocky spur overlooking
the holy way that runs
along the western side of
Wadi Farasa. Some
believe it depicts the god
Dusares, others the

goddess Al Uzza. In
either case, it would be
one of the few known
figurative representations
of a Nabatean divinity.

122-123 The Garden
Tomb is a mysterious
monument; it could not
have been a burial place,
therebeing no trace of
loculi or graves, but the
suggestion that it was a
triclinium does not
seem very convincing
either, particularly
because there are no
triclinial beds inside.
It may have been a
temple, built to "protect"
the nearby cistern.

THE GARDEN TOMB

Although at times quite treacherous the path never becomes dangerous and offers magnificent views over the Wadi Farasa valley and, in the distance, over Wadi Nmeir and Wadi Thughra. It also provides an opportunity to see the monuments below from an unusual angle: the façade of the Roman Soldier Tomb, a cistern and adjacent chamber (now without its roof), with niches in the walls. The latter two structures can be reached directly along a very steep path, but it is far safer to follow the main route which, in a few minutes and after some last bends, will bring you to one of Petra's loveliest monuments. Known as the "Garden Tomb" it is not large, nor architecturally elaborate, but it is dug in an extraordinary position on a promontory that juts out over the valley. The backdrop to this splendid setting is the Petra valley in the distance and a blue sky that contrasts splendidly with the warm colors of the sandstone. The Tomb consists of an elegant, simple portico with two columns *in antis* leading to a sort of vestibule, which then opens onto a simple, totally unadorned square chamber.

The structure owes its charming name to the fact that when the 19th-century visitors saw it, the courtyard in front was partially covered with soil fallen from above and full of oleander bushes and other plants. Actually, this was not the intention of its builders, who did not conceive the hypogeum as a tomb. It was probably a temple, similar to that dug in the el Barid Siq, described later, although some interpret it as a triclinial chamber. The age of the monument is also disputed; some

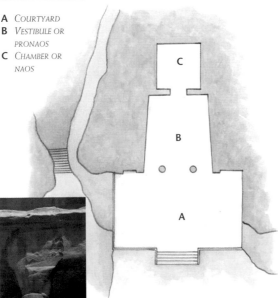

123 bottom left and top right The pictures show details of the lovely façade in antis of the Garden Tomb and clearly show the use of the characteristic Nabatean capital.

123 bottom right The chamber opposite the great cistern – perhaps a triclinial chamber – was covered with a barrel vault, quite a rare architectural feature in Petra.

A COURTYARD
B VESTIBULE OR PRONAOS
C CHAMBER OR NAOS

suggest that it dates from the reign of Aretas IV (8 BC-40 AD) or the second half of the first century AD, but according to others it may have been part of the nearby Roman Soldier complex. A great wall stands to the right of the courtyard in front of the portico; to discover its purpose you must climb a steep flight of steps that leads to the edge of a huge cistern (now dry), more than 60 feet long and half as wide. The wall is its south side. At the opposite end is the chamber, mentioned above, with walls containing niches. This was once covered with a barrel vault and must have served as a *triclinium*.

A   *MAIN FUNERARY*
    CHAMBER
B   *SECONDARY FUNERARY*
    CHAMBER
C   *LOCULI*
D   *COURTYARD*
D   *TRICLINIUM*

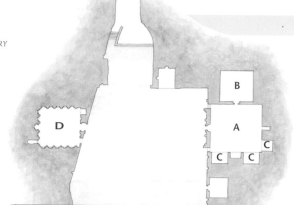

THE ROMAN SOLDIER TOMB

A flight of steps descends to the left of the Garden Temple towards the bottom of the gradually widening Wadi Farasa valley. After a hundred yards or so, the processional way opens in a vast courtyard, partially dug into the sides of the two opposite mountains.
The great façade of the Roman Soldier Tomb is carved in the rock wall to the left, facing west. Of dignified elegance, this is the most famous example of the

124-125 Seen from above, it is easier to gauge the amount of excavation required to create the courtyard in front of the Roman Soldier Tomb. The hypogeum situated above the façade is also clearly visible here.

124 left Although the façade of the Roman Soldier Tomb is obviously of classical inspiration, typically Nabatean elements such as the capitals and the half-pillars with quarter columns continued to be adopted.

"Roman Classical style" introduced to Petra after it was conquered by the emperor Trajan. The front resembles that of a tetrastyle temple. It is flanked by the customary half-pillars with leaning quarter columns and the portal is framed between two half-columns. The capitals appear to be in the usual Nabatean style, but are greatly eroded by the rain and wind. The entablature, devoid of a frieze, supports a low tympanum placed against a rectangular parapet on which perhaps were three acroterions; the stone is so worn, however, that this hypothesis is very uncertain. Above the portal is a tympanum with a Doric frieze extremely similar to that of the Urn Tomb. The truly striking features of

124

125 *The Roman Soldier Tomb was most certainly destined for an important figure and his family. On the basis of the type of armor worn by the bas-relief statue that adorns the niche in the central intercolumn (center picture), he is presumed to be a high-ranking officer of the Roman army or even an imperial legate. According to this interpretation the two men represented in the side niches (pictures top and bottom) would have been his sons. The design of the façade, which contains motifs typical of Greco-Roman funerary architecture, suggests a date around the first decades of the second century AD.*

this tomb are the three unusual niches high up, in each of the intercolumns. Framed by a simple cornice with a smooth entablature, they were adorned with numerous bas-relief statues. The central one, unfortunately headless and without its legs, depicts a man in a heroic pose and wearing elaborate armor, similar in design to that used by Roman soldiers. It most certainly portrays a high-ranking figure and the statues in the side niches, apparently wearing short military-style tunics, are presumed to portray the sons of the deceased. Traces of plaster are still visible in the folds of the cloaks which would suggest that the statues were originally richly colored.

Above the façade, to the left, is a deep rectangular hollow, probably that of a grave demolished during the construction of the new tomb. Lower

down, to the right, is a row of four recesses, of unknown purpose (perhaps niches housing numerous baetyli), and two obelisks are traced in very low relief on the right-hand wall of the façade. Inside, the tomb consists of two simple funerary chambers; some arcosolium loculi are dug along the walls of the first, in which the bodies were laid, wrapped in shrouds or enclosed in wooden sarcophagi (this too is still open to debate). The courtyard that lies in front of the tomb was created by partially excavating the sides of the mountain and levelling the bottom of the valley. To do this the builders had to construct a strong

126 top Niches and conduits for water are found all around the Roman Soldier Tomb.

126 center The groove above the three doors that lead to the triclinium supported the pitch of the colonnaded portico roof, thus making room for the three windows that illuminated the inside chamber.

retention wall and, very probably, force the course of the *wadi* through a vaulted tunnel. However small the seasonal stream may have been, its flow increases dramatically during the violent winter and spring rains. This mass of water, no longer properly controlled, has over the centuries caused serious damage to the monumental complex. The front of the hypogeum immediately opposite the tomb, which is totally devoid of architectural elements, shows its effect. The doorways have been misshapen by

erosion and the interior is also severely ruined. Nevertheless, the vast square chamber is one of the most fascinating in all Petra; the walls, with their magnificent colored veining, are remarkable in themselves and are decorated with a harmonious alternation of fluted pilaster strips and niches dug in the intercolumns. The elegant half-columns – surmounted by capitals that seem to represent a new syncretism of Tuscan, Ionic and Nabatean orders – sustain an entablature devoid of a frieze, but which

must originally have been covered with multicolored stuccowork. Plaster moldings also framed each niche, as is revealed by grooves that housed the wooden corbels used as reinforcement. The low unbroken dais running around three sides of the room proves that this was a triclinium. This chamber, with such refined decoration, is the only surviving example of its kind in Petra and is a true exception. During inspections conducted in the early twentieth century, the German archaeologist W. von Bachmann

126 bottom This imaginary recon-struction, inspired by those of W. von Bachmann and I. Browning, gives an idea of what the

monumental complex of tomb, triclinium and large courtyard surrounded on three sides by porticoes must originally have looked like.

126-127 and 127 bottom The triclinium is a large square-plan chamber, measuring approximately 35 feet on all sides. Refined banquets were held

here in honor of the deceased and his forefathers. With its fluted pilaster strips, entablature and niches, this is the only known internal chamber so

magnificently decorated in Petra. While observing what has survived, you must picture the walls as they once were, plastered and frescoed.

(on the basis of the remains of walls still visible *in situ* and the description given on the front of the Turkamaniya Tomb) formulated the hypothesis that the courtyard between the tomb and the *triclinium* was surrounded on three sides by a colonnaded portico. His guess has been proven right by the latest studies of Nabatean funerary architecture, which confirm the close link between tombs, porticoed courtyards and *triclinia*.

THE RENAISSANCE TOMB

As it moves away from the Roman Soldier Tomb, the processional path continues for a short stretch as a flight of steps before turning into a sandy track, only in parts cut in the rock. On the left side of the gorge, to the south, is a wadi dug deep in the spurs of Jebel al Najr. Those with 20 minutes to spare and plenty of breath should make a detour to a rather interesting but little-visited tomb. Known simply as the al Najr Tomb, it has a very well-preserved classical façade that closely resembles the Roman Soldier Tomb. Dating from the same period, it differs in that there are no niches in the intercolumns; as a result, it appears more compact, less vertical and very similar to the front of a tetrastyle temple.

At the point where the Wadi Farasa valley opens unexpectedly, the eye is drawn to a particularly elegant,

westward-facing façade on the right. This well-proportioned structure is known as the Renaissance Tomb and, on observation, it is easy to understand why. The front is framed with the customary half-pillars with quarter columns and supports an entablature with a smooth frieze and a low tympanum, adorned with three urn-shaped acroterions.

The doorway is the most striking feature of the composition and resembles the pure architectural designs of the Italian renaissance. The inner cornice of the door is of the standard type but the outer one presents the usual half-pillars with Nabatean capitals supporting not a normal entablature but an open pediment, consisting of a segmental arch with three urn-shaped acroterions resting on the extrados. The whole is very similar to the Tomb of Sextius Florentinus and, for this reason, it is thought to be from the first half of the second century AD.

THE BROKEN PEDIMENT TOMB

A short distance beyond the Renaissance Tomb the Wadi Farasa valley widens further and is full of rounded sandstone outcrops and large oleander bushes. The surrounding mountain slopes contain numerous façades, most of the step type, and the ever-present channelling which

129 top The dignified and austere Broken Pediment Tomb stands on a terrace approached up a flight of steps; the adjacent room, altered over the centuries and used as stables, must have been a triclinium.

129 center left The entrance to the Broken Pediment Tomb is preceded by a flight of steps dug in the rock; unfortunately, the architrave of the door is seriously damaged, but it must have been of the standard kind, with a simple entablature. The two slits in the outer intercolumns seem unrelated to the original project and probably date from a time when the tomb was turned into a dwelling or stables. In the past, this was the fate of many of Petra's rock structures.

carried rainwater to cisterns cleverly hidden in the subsoil. On the same side as the Renaissance Tomb and just a few dozen yards from it, is one of the stylistically most successful pieces of architecture in Petra. Carved in a rocky ledge, facing north, the Broken Pediment Tomb shows that the Nabatean builders managed to totally resolve the sharp contrast between formal schemes imported from the Hellenized west and the local passion for abundant decorative elements. The façade is divided by four half-pillars with leaning quarter columns, surmounted by a simple entablature sustaining a broken pediment. This same scheme was observed in the Bab el Siq Triclinium and in the Corinthian Tomb, but total equilibrium is achieved here, far from the muddle of lintels, cornices and short half-pillars that needlessly weigh some compositions down.

The Broken Pediment Tomb

must have belonged to a highly influential family and stands at the top of a flight of steps, above the path. The front is preceded by a large terrace, in which are dug two tanks, one octagonal and the other square. On the right-hand wall inside the tomb are four loculi and the marks for the digging of more, never executed. Work was obviously suspended quite suddenly, but why remains a mystery.

The sides of Jebel Attuf just beyond the Broken Pediment Tomb are dotted with rock façades in tiered rows, as seen in the Outer Siq. Continuing on you come to a fork, at a point that affords a sweeping view of the valley occupied by the city of Petra. Turning left you can quickly reach Kasr el Bint and the nearby refreshment kiosk; if you go right you can round the outermost spurs of Jebel Attuf and the path leads in 20 minutes or so to the mouth of the Outer Siq, near the Theater.

129 center right Wind erosion has given a bizarre appearance to this hypogeum along Wadi Farasa, almost certainly an ancient rock dwelling.

129 bottom The spurs of Jebel Attuf in the lower Wadi Farasa valley are full of tombs – most of the "step" type – aligned in rows.

Petra

130 top The unusual Eagle Monument is situated near the Nabatean tunnel, at the mouth of the Little Siq.

130 bottom Long stretches of the Little Siq, or Wadi Muthlim, look like a fissure eroded between the sheer high rock walls by water.

131 The sides of the Little Siq are lined with remarkable natural formations and splendid banks of polychrome sandstone.

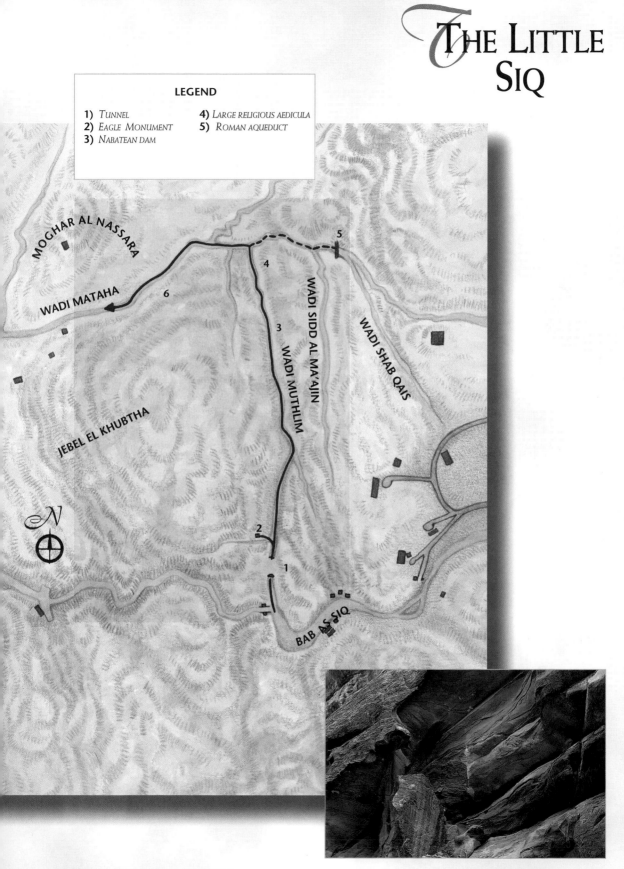

THE LITTLE SIQ

LEGEND

1) TUNNEL
2) EAGLE MONUMENT
3) NABATEAN DAM
4) LARGE RELIGIOUS AEDICULA
5) ROMAN AQUEDUCT

MOGHAR AL NASSARA

WADI MATAHA

JEBEL EL KHUBTHA

WADI SIDD AL MA'AJIN

WADI MUTHLIM

WADI SHAB QAIS

BAB AS SIQ

N

132 top left and top right The splendid coloring of the rocks makes the Little Siq a particular favorite of photographers.

THE LITTLE SIQ

132 bottom left
The photograph shows what remains of the barrier built inside the Little Siq. The foundations of a defense wall and what must have been a guard post stand near the rocky spur visible high on the left.

The Little Siq, or Wadi Muthlim, is one of the most spectacular yet least known wonders of Petra. This relative anonymity is due to the objective difficulty involved in the trek along the riverbed and the length of the journey; as a result the following itinerary is for expert hikers, equipped with the proper footwear and plenty of water. We recommend against undertaking the descent of the *wadi* during the rainy season or whenever violent thunderstorms precede the planned excursion, as the gorge may be invaded without prior warning by flash floods.

On the last stretch, where the *wadi* becomes a narrow fracture, great

attention must be paid to falling boulders; this is not uncommon and is often caused by goats grazing on the slopes of Jebel al Khubtha above.

Only the first part of the journey – to the so-called Eagle Monument – can be followed by anyone taking a little care. First leave the main road before the bridge to the Interior Siq; note that some stelae and obelisks, dating from the reign of Malchus II (40-70 AD), are visible on the wall opposite the modern dam. An inscription discovered here bears the Nabatean name of Petra: Reqem.

Following the Tunnel to the Muthlim – to the right of which stands a *"djin"* block, decorated at the top with an Assyrian frieze – presents no particular difficulties, as there is enough light to see any obstacles.

Once on the other side follow the riverbed for about 164 feet; here it is enclosed between two slightly sloping walls dug into the sandstone; then climb to the left.

The surrounding area abounds with Nabatean remains, although they are not easy to see: niches, stelae, obelisks and, above all, the Eagle Monument, a votive niche probably dating from Roman times; in the

132 bottom right The waters of Wadi Mousa are deviated through the 280-foot-long Nabatean tunnel into Wadi Muthlim.

This impressive hydraulic project is thought to have been completed shortly before Petra was annexed to the Roman Empire.

132-133 The Eagle Monument is carved a hundred yards from the mouth of the Nabatean tunnel. Given the subject of this bas-relief, the monument probably dates from the period of Roman domain.

133 top A few yards from the point where Wadi Muthlim flows into the wide Wadi Mataha valley, the sides of the gorge are dotted with niches and baetyli; inscriptions found indicate that Dusares, Al Uzza and "all the gods" were worshipped here.

middle of the niche stands the figure of a bird of prey with outspread wings.

Back on the riverbed the most adventurous will turn away from the Tunnel and start to descend Wadi Muthlim. It takes at least 40 minutes to reach the edge of the gorge, but the beauty of the place will inspire constant stopping. Indeed this itinerary, which in the near future may be equipped with steps and handrails,

is particularly spectacular from a naturalistic and scenographic point of view, thanks to the glowing colors and uneven formation of the surrounding rocks. In addition, the route does contain some interesting archaeological discoveries. First, it is illuminating to observe the engineering brilliance of the Nabateans, who managed to exploit the complex orography of the region and find a new course for the Wadi

Mousa.

However narrow and difficult, the gorge constituted a possible route of access to the city, with the inhabitants of Petra well aware of the danger. So, approximately three-quarters of the way along, where the mountain walls become increasingly higher and close to one another, they built an effective barrier, traces of which are still clearly visible. Two holes were dug at a certain height above the river on both

*134 top With a large
number of aediculae,
niches and baetyli dug
into the rock walls, the
mouth of the Little Siq
is an open-air
sanctuary, probably
linked to the worship of
water.*

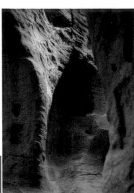

*134-135 The Wadi
Muthlim gorge – or
Little Siq – opens into
the wide Wadi Mataha
valley right opposite the
Moghar al Nassara
heights, another area
with many rock tombs
and cisterns.*

*135 top left and bottom
The spurs of Jebel el-
Kubtha lie on the
orographic left of
Wadi Mataha;
numerous rock
dwellings and an
aqueduct can be seen on
the mountainside.*

*135 center left The
most striking rock
structure of the open-
air sanctuary in
Wadi Mataha is this
large religious
aedicula, carved inside
a huge pothole.*

sides of the fissure; two protruding
stone ledges were fixed to these, and
an arch was set on them, beneath a
wall which must originally have been
about 10 feet high. The span of the
arch was then closed by a strong grill,
through which the river could pass
even when flooded, but which proved
an impassable obstacle to invaders.

Moreover, the rocky spur above
bears the remains of a wall and a

tower, perhaps used by guards. Now
that the arch has collapsed and only a
part of the barrier remains suspended
above one of the ledges, this defense
system may seem of little account, but
when it was built it must have been of
mortal effect. No enemy arriving in
this natural bottleneck would have had
a chance to report back what he had
just discovered.

A few dozen yards farther on, the

"Little Siq" becomes a cleft fashioned
by the water into fantastic shapes; in
some parts no more than 24 inches
wide, enclosed between sheer walls
that block out the view of the sky.
The light that reaches the bottom of
the chasm is like that of an aquarium
and the scene becomes increasingly
impressive.

Suddenly, numerous niches with
carvings appear in the multicolored

135 top right The
Wadi Mataha gorge is
spanned by the
beautifully-positioned
arch of an aqueduct that
brought the water of
Wadi Mousa to Petra;
the arch probably dates
from Roman times.

More determined hikers can
prolong this itinerary by turning
right at the point where the Little Siq
joins Wadi Mataha. Initially, you
follow the normally dry bed of Wadi
Mataha, passing (on the right) the
fissure of Wadi Sidd al-Ma'ajin, a
gorge that runs parallel to the Little
Siq. Not far ahead, high up, you will
notice the daring arch of a Roman
aqueduct that used to bring the water
collected by the Al Birka reservoir to
Petra. Once past the arch, go up
Wadi Shab Qais, the right-hand
tributary of Wadi Mataha, and in less
than two hours you will reach the
village of Wadi Mousa, near the Petra
Forum Hotel.

135 bottom right One of
the votive aediculae carved
in the Little Siq is topped
with a crescent moon, a
symbol often associated
with the worship of Al
Uzza. A large temple in
Petra is known to have
been dedicated to this
goddess but has not yet
been identified.

rock walls, demonstrating that this
was considered a holy place. Shortly
before the gorge opens in the wide
luminous Wadi Mataha valley is a
last thrill: two half-columns,
surmounted by a massive architrave
and framing another two smaller half-
columns (this time connected by a
curved front), are sculpted within a
vast rectangular cavity. The central
niche probably contained the image
of a god.

   Once out of the Little Siq (in an
area dotted with rock structures)
follow the course of the Wadi
Mataha, which bends to the left; you
will soon come to the House of
Dorotheos, then the tomb of Sextius
Florentinus and from here, the center
of Petra.

Petra

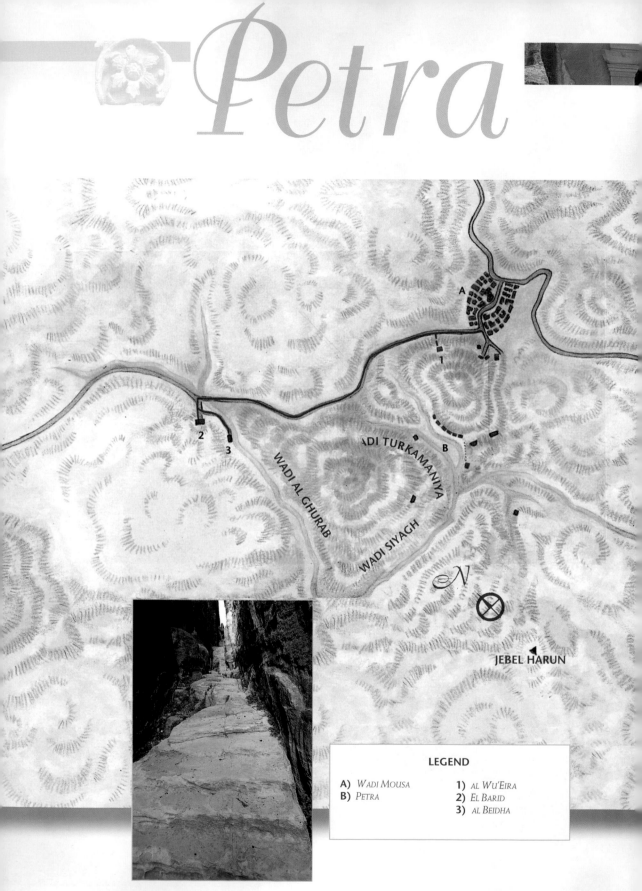

WADI TURKAMANIYA

WADI AL GHURAB

WADI SIYAGH

N

JEBEL HARUN

LEGEND

A) *Wadi Mousa*
B) *Petra*

1) *al Wu'Eira*
2) *El Barid*
3) *al Beidha*

EL BARID (LITTLE PETRA) AND AL BEIDHA

136 Numerous flights of steps cut in the rock have been conserved at el Barid, also known as "Little Petra". Some of these lead to reservoirs and channelling, others to small open-air sanctuaries.

137 top This fine porticoed façade with two columns in antis is carved inside the lovely el Barid Siq.

137 bottom Al Beidha is considered one of the oldest settlements in the entire Middle East. Some of the structures discovered here date from the initial phases of the seventh millennium BC.

EL BARID (LITTLE PETRA) AND AL BEIDHA

138 left El Barid was
Petra's main trading
suburb to the east, and
this is one of its most
famous monuments.

138 top right The Siq,
a narrow gorge
overlooked by numerous
rock structures, must
have been el Barid's
main "thoroughfare."

139 bottom right
With just a few tombs
and so many cisterns,
triclinia, biclinia,
dwellings and hypogea,
possibly used to store
merchandise, el Barid
was, more than
anything else, a large
emporium.

139 Carved at the
entrance to the el Barid
Siq - in a similar position
to that of the Khasneh —
is the elegant pedimented
façade of a monument
thought to be a temple
maybe built during the
prosperous reign of Aretas
IV (8 BC - 40 AD).

Petra is a vast archaeological area, literally covered with rock monuments, which are often situated some distance from the ancient center. The valleys and peaks of the surrounding mountains are full of unexpected thrills. Within a couple of miles of Colonnade Street, taken as the imaginary geographical center of the area, you will frequently dedicate half a day or more to a visit to a small but charming village situated a couple of miles from the village of Wadi Mousa, el Barid. This can actually be considered a suburb of Petra and can be reached on foot from the Visitors' Center, along the asphalt road to Shawbak; the scenery is stunning, but the hike takes at least

come across tombs, votive niches, flights of steps, cisterns and channels. The eight itineraries thus far proposed are not intended to be exhaustive, but have been drawn up on the basis of an essentially practical requirement: they cover all the main monuments, are relatively easy to follow, do not take too long, and allow you to form a fairly comprehensive picture of the Nabatean settlement. Those with several days available and who wish to explore the site thoroughly, should buy a detailed map of Petra or engage an authorized guide. Thorough exploration of the area will offer fascinating, often unusual and breathtaking views and groups of tombs hewn into secondary gorges, but you should know that nothing will compare with what has been presented so far. Those who are satisfied with what has already been described can

two hours and so it is best to hire a vehicle – possibly with an escort – or take a taxi (either way, it will take no longer than 15 minutes). The same place can also be reached from the center of Petra by following the Wadi Turkamaniya, but the route is far longer, more difficult and tiring. Before reaching el Barid you can visit the crusader castle of Al Wu'aira; this stands on the left side of the road approximately half a mile from Wadi Mousa, perched in a formidable position, but it is by no means easy to see. Reduced mostly to a heap of ruins, it is nevertheless of some interest. Surrounded on all sides by steep ravines, it can be reached along a path that climbs to an unusual chamber hewn into a solid rocky spur. The original drawbridge that provided access to the fortress has been

replaced with a footbridge. Al Wu'aira, which the Crusaders called Li Vaux Moise, was erected around 1116 at the wish of King Baldwin I of Jerusalem, as part of the system of defense erected to control trade along the road from Cairo to Damascus. Besieged without success by the Muslim armies first in 1144 and then in 1158, it was eventually overrun in 1189, after Saladin had defeated the Christian forces in the battle of Hattin. Al Wu'aira was the last Crusader outpost to surrender. Occupied by an Ayyubite garrison until the early 13th century, it was eventually abandoned.
Turn left at the turn-off for Shawbak; after a few yards on the right you will notice steps cut into the rock. The most curious will stop for a while and climb up to admire the largest known Nabatean cistern in the Petra area.

140 top left This roomy
underground chamber,
excavated inside the el
Barid Siq, was a
triclinium: merchants
would gather here in the
cool shade, feasting and
negotiating the price of
their wares.

140 bottom left The
first clearing in the el
Barid Siq, once used as
a caravanserai, is
dominated by the façade
of a rock structure with
two columns in antis,
almost certainly a
temple.

140-141 The large
chamber visible at the
top left is known as the
"Painted House." Its
walls and ceiling
display extensive pieces
of fresco decoration
dating from the
Nabatean period.
Presumably, all the

rock dwellings in Petra
were originally
embellished with mural
paintings, regrettably
most are now des-
troyed. Near the house
are other dwellings and
several triclinia.
Outside the funeral
context, triclinia were

the equivalent of modern
dining rooms. Many of
them, at least in el
Barid, may therefore
have been "restaurants,"
public places similar to
the thermopolia
discovered in Pompeii,
also with triclinial
beds.

Nearby you will also see considerable
terracing built by the ancient
inhabitants of the area to increase the
surface of land for farming. Continuing
along the road you will come to a
place where you can park the car. In a
scene of surreal beauty, a clearly visible
path descends towards el Barid, once
an outpost of Petra and an important
caravanserai; here is where the
caravans going back and forth between
the Mediterranean coasts and Arabia
stopped and commodities destined for
the markets of Petra were stored.

The valley continues to narrow,
until it starts to look like a miniature
Siq; not surprisingly, this is its very
name: Siq el Barid. At the mouth of the
narrow gorge, a short flight of steps
leads to the entrance of a rather small

but very elegant and still well-preserved tomb. Actually, not all agree as
to the true function of this structure,
which can be dated to the first half of
the first century AD, and some believe
it was really a rock temple. El Barid is
usually a solitary and silent place and
entering the Siq becomes a vaguely
mysterious experience. Multicolored
walls of polished stone, at times so
close to one another as to leave just
the bare space needed for passage,
break up the noise of footsteps in a
play of echoes, as the light becomes
increasingly watery. Natural clearings
suddenly open all along the passage,
the walls of which are riddled with
niches, façades, channels and cisterns;
here and there steep flights of steps
lead to a "high place", where the
Nabateans worshipped their gods.

141 top left The
photograph shows one
of the circular
structures uncovered on
the archaeological site
of al Beidha. The roofs
of these Neolithic
dwellings were made of
straw and mud applied
to a framework of
branches and supported
by a tall pole placed at
the center. As they
leaned against each
other, their walls
supported one another.
In many cases the
internal walls were
covered with a plaster
made of fine dry mud.

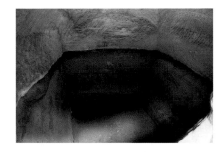

sort of transverse flute; another, which could be a representation of Eros, is armed with bow and arrows. Even though the colors are rather faded, the ceiling is of great interest because it is one of the few surviving examples of Nabataean wall decoration.

Approximately half a mile southeast of el Barid, in an alluvial plain overlooking Wadi al Ghurab, stand the remains of a prehistoric village, known as Al Beidha (the white one). The archaeological excavations of the site, considered one of the oldest in all the Middle East, have so far uncovered nine levels, corresponding to as many phases of inhabitation, from the Mesolithic to the early Neolithic. At the time the region was at least partially covered with juniper and oak woods, in which lived gazelles, camels, wild goats, jackals, boars and numerous other animals; the inhabitants of Al Beidha were given over to gathering edible vegetables and hunting, activities later replaced by the cultivation of barley and

141 top right El Barid also has spectacular and mysterious-looking flights of steps carved into the sandstone. Some lead to cisterns and channelling systems, others to holy places situated on high.

shepherding. In addition to the stone and bone tools and the numerous millstones found in the area, other products, such as obsidian and sea shells – obviously imported from far-off regions— were also found. In the archaeological area, the foundations of some basement houses with a round plan, dating from 6800 BC, are noteworthy; the rectangular or square plan dwellings are more recent, but still date from the second half of the seventh century BC. Not far from the settlement, a necropolis has been discovered, which revealed funerary customs similar to those of other sites of the same period, in which the adults were buried decapitated.

Al Beidha was definitively abandoned, perhaps following climatic changes, around 6000 BC; the Nabateans, who occupied the region much later, terraced the site for farming purposes and for this reason the study of most of the surface levels of the Neolithic village is extremely difficult.

It is very likely that merchants from afar used to stop in these pleasantly cool and sheltered spaces; here they rested, feasted and conducted business.

Actually, the surrounding rock structures are mostly *triclinium* rooms as well as true and proper dwellings, whereas the number of tombs is rather small. In the first of these caravanserai there is a splendid façade that presents itself as a portico in antis, the two columns of which were restored a few years ago; in the second is a biclinium, reached via a narrow concrete walkway, which inside has a still-preserved ceiling frescoed with vine-shoots, racemes, flowers, birds of various species and cupids.

One of these, identified by some as the young Pan, is busy playing a

141 bottom right Numerous querns can still be seen at Al Beidha. These simple but effective tools were used by the Neolithic peoples to make flour, and the wheat grown on the surrounding heights represented one of the main sources of nourishment.

GLOSSARY

ACROTERION: a decoration in the form of a vase, palmette or other, placed at the apex and two ends of a pediment.

AEDICULA: kind of niche which usually hosted the statue of a divinity.

AMAZON: in Greek mythology, a female warrior, close to the goddess Artemis.

ANICONICAL: not allowing the use of images.

ARCHITRAVE: the same as lintel; horizontal stone resting over door, window or columns

ARCOSOLIUM: a niche with an arched roof, usually excavated inside tombs and catacombs, that contained the body of the deceased.

ATTIC: the raised level above the cornice of a building or the entablature of a temple, serving an ornamental function.

BAETYLUS: the non-figured representation of the Nabatean gods, usually in the form of a truncated pyramid, a cube, parallelepiped, cylinder or, sometimes, a hemisphere. Literally, the term means "house of the deity".

BICLINIUM: a banqueting chamber similar to the triclinium, but with just two triclinial beds, usually set parallel to one another.

CARAVANSERAI: great court where caravans put up for the night.

CELLA: the inner chamber of a temple.

CONFRATERNITY: the same as brotherood.

CORNUCOPIA: a vase shaped like a long horn and filled with herbs, flowers and fruit, a symbol of fertility and plenty.

ENTABLATURE: a structure resting on columns, consisting of an architrave, frieze and cornice.

EXTRADOS: moulding round exterior of arch.

FIRMAN: an edict or permit issued by Turkish sovereigns.

FRIEZE: an elongated painted or carved architectural decoration.

HELLENISM: the period in history between the death of Alexander the Great (323 BC) and the Roman conquest of Egypt (31 BC), during which Greek art was influenced by the Orient and adopted a marked tendency towards realism and effective representation.

IN ANTIS: this is used for a temple façade with two or more columns and two pillars at the ends of the projecting walls.

INTERCOLUMN: the space between two adjacent columns.

ISIS: the most important goddess of ancient Egypt, representing rebirth, fertility and love.

LOCULUS: locule, burial niche.

METOPE: this is the space between the triglyphs of a Doric entablature, usually adorned with bas-relief carvings or simple disks.

NIKE (PL. NIKAI): a Greek goddess, daughter of Zeus, the personification of victory and usually portrayed winged.

NYMPHAEUM: in the classical world, an apsed construction with niches and a large central fountain, often adorned with statues.

PATERA: a low, wide bowl-shaped cup used in antiquity during libations.

PEDIMENT: a triangular element, with two sloping sides, used to crown buildings, doors, niches or windows.

PERIPTERAL: this term is used to describe a building surrounded by a row of columns.

PERISTYLE: a portico with columns surrounding a courtyard.

PRONAOS: the covered space between the colonnade on a façade and the interior of the temple or building.

RACEMO: ornamental motif consisting of foliage arranged in volutes.

id Roberts

SUBSTRUCTURE: a masonry structure, sometimes underground, that constitutes the support base for the construction above.

TEMENOS: open-air precinct, a holy enclosure, where ceremonies in honor of the deities were held.

THOLOS: a circular temple with a conical roof.

TETRASTYLE: building or temple with four columns on the front.

TRANSENNA: the wooden or marble parapet that divided the presbytery from the nave in early Christian churches.

TRICLINIUM: a banqueting chamber, with three beds arranged around the walls, at which the diners lay on one side.

TRIGLYPH: a decorative motif in a Doric entablature applied in alternation with the metopes and consisting of a small tablet with two central grooves.

TYCHE: Greek goddess of good fortune, whose attributes were the cornucopia and the ear of corn.

TYMPANUM: the triangular area between the sloping sides of a pediment and the architrave, it may be smooth, have relief decoration or contain group sculptures.

VESTIBULE: the portico that precedes the cella of a temple.

BIBLIOGRAPHY

Avi-Yonah M., *Petra*, in Enciclopedia dell'Arte Antica Treccani, Rome 1961.

Ballantine J., *The Life of David Roberts*, Edinburgh 1866.

Browning I., *Petra*, London 1982.

Gagos T. (edited by), *The carbonized papyri from Petra*, University of Michigan 1994.

Guzzo M.G.A. and Schneider E.E., *Petra*, Milan 1997.

Harding Lankester G., *The Antiquities of Jordan*, London 1959.

Howard T., *Treks and climbs in the Mountains of Wadi Rum and Petra*, Jordan, 1987.

Keiser H., *Petra dei Nabatei*, Torino 1972.

Laborde, L.de, *Voyage de l'Arabie Pétrée*, Paris 1830.

Lyttlelton M., *Baroque architecture in Classical antiquity*, London 1974.

Maqsood R., *Petra: a travellers' guide*, Lebanon 1996.

McKenzie J., *The Architecture of Petra*, Oxford 1990.

Rostovtzeff M., *Città carovaniere*, Bari 1971.

Piccirillo M., *The Mosaics of Jordan*, Jordan 1991.

Stephens J. L., *Incidents of Travel in Egypt, Arabia Petraea, and the Holy Land*, New York 1837.

Taylor J., *Petra*, London 1993.

Taylor J., *Petra, l'impero delle rocce*, in Archeo n.134, Novara 1996.

Zayadine F. (edited by), *Petra and the Caravan Cities*, Amman 1990.

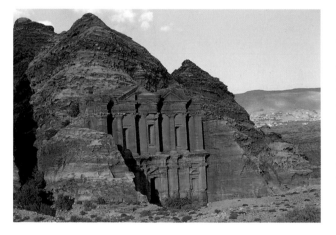

144 Rocks stripped bare by the elements and silence broken only by the whistling wind – the Deir rises, majestic in its solitude, on a cliff overlooking the ancient Nabatean capital. Forgotten for centuries, Petra is still shrouded in the mystery of the past. If you wish to fully experience its bewitching charm, you must be able to listen to this secret silence.

PHOTOGRAPHIC REFERENCES